A Floral
Grimoire

About the Author

Patricia Telesco (Trish) has been a part of the Neopagan community for over 30 years. During that time, she penned many memorable titles, including *Victorian Grimoire, Goddess in my Pocket, Spinning Spells; Weaving Wonders*, and the first edition of *Kitchen Witch's Cookbook.*

During her speaking engagements across the U.S., Trish met many wise people working behind the scenes who blessed her with down-to-earth perspectives for going forward with books and life. Along the way, cooking at festivals led to writing more about culinary topics. The result has been very happy bellies for family and friends alike.

Food is love; food is hospitality. Food changes life, and life changes food.

A Floral Grimoire

Plant Charms, Spells, Recipes, and Rituals

Patricia Telesco

Chicago, Illinois

First Printing. 2024.

Paperback ISBN: 978-1-959883-32-6
Hardcover ISBN: 978-1-959883-73-9
Library of Congress Control Number on file.

Cover design by Wycke Malliway.
Edited by Marcus Robertson.
Typesetting by Gianna Rini.

Published by:
Crossed Crow Books, LLC
6934 N Glenwood Ave, Suite C
Chicago, IL 60626
www.crossedcrowbooks.com

Printed in the United States of America.

Other Books by the Author

A Victorian Grimoire, Crossed Crow Books (2023)
Kitchen Witch's Guide to Magickal Tools, New Page Books (2006)
Cakes and Ale For The Pagan Soul, Crossing Press (2005)
The Kitchen Witch Companion, Citadel (2005)
Which Witch Is Which?, New Page Books (2004)
A Kitchen Witch's Cookbook, Llewellyn (2002)
How To Be A Wicked Wtich, Atria (2001)
An Enchanted Life, New Page Books (2001)
Cat Magic, Destiny Books (1999)
365 Goddess, HarperOne (1998)
Goddess in My Pocket, HarperOne (1998)

Forthcoming
from Crossed Crow Books

A Victorian Flower Oracle
The Urban Pagan
The Witch's Book of Wisdom
Spinning Spell Weaving Wonders
The Teen Book of Shadows
Advanced Wicca
Your Book of Shadows
Folkways
Future Telling
Ghosts, Spirits, and Hauntings
Magical Places
Labyrinth Walking
The Herbal Arts
The Wiccan Book of Ceremonies and Rituals
A Little Book of Mirror Magick
A Little Book of Love Magick
Gardening with the Goddess
Mastering Candle Magick
Money Magick

For Scarlett, who now understands the value of sippy cups in hot tubs. Also for all my friends and readers, who are truly the flowers of The God/dess's garden.

Contents

Chapter 1
Witchy Wildflowers
and Plants · 4

Chapter 2
Green Magic · 23

Chapter 3
Magical Gardens · 43

Chapter 4
Edible Petals and
Blossoming Beverages · 66

Chapter 5
Aromatic Magic
and Handcrafts · 93

Chapter 6
Petaled Psychism:
Floromancy and Botanomancy · 117

Chapter 7
Spicy Spells and Charms · 143

Foreword

As a lover of books of any kind and a Witch, my shelves are full to overflowing with tomes of wonder, insight, and information. Several of those on my shelf have been written by the wonderful author, Patricia Telesco.

I have a copy of the original version of *A Floral Grimoire* by Patricia which is well-thumbed and full of sticky notes marking pages of interest. I have used my copy of this fabulous book for reference when working spells, creating magic, or writing my own books on many occasions over the years. In fact, it was this book that introduced me to the art of divination with flowers. So I was extremely pleased to hear about it being re-published by Crossed Crow Books.

Working with herbs, plants, and flowers for magical purposes is at the heart of many practices for Witches and magical folk. Every plant—in fact, every natural item—has an energy field and it is by tapping into that energy we can discover what magic they can help us with. Mother Nature provides us with a whole host of items to use for free in our spells and rituals. From the humble blade of grass up to the most exotic flower, each one brings magic with it.

The idea of working magic with flora and fauna is not a new or modern one. People across the world have been using them in folk magic practices going back hundreds, probably thousands of years. We can learn from those original folk and how they connected with that magic.

For me, the root (no pun intended) of this is *connection*. We need to be connected to the energy of the land we live on and that extends to the plants and flowers. Reach out to the area around you, to your own garden, your street, your town, or city. Make a connection with the soil beneath your feet, the soil beneath the concrete, and way down below the foundations. Open yourself up to the energy the plants provide when you are walking down the road or in your local park. There is magical energy everywhere.

Nature provides so much for us to learn from, along with energy to guide and support us. Each plant and flower has a spirit within that can be connected with to help not just with our magical workings, but for insight and guidance too. Make friends with the plants, open up to them, and build a relationship—you won't be disappointed with the results.

A Floral Grimoire takes you on a journey that begins with the history and foundation of working magic with plants, which is truly fascinating. There are suggestions and guidance to set you on the right track to commune with the spirits of plants and to help you build a relationship with them. Patricia also gives good practical advice on how to work with your plants and deal with the mundane tasks within your own gardens, all of which are necessary if you want to really make this work for you.

Patricia's book contains correspondences, suggested phases for working magic, seasonal workings, and good foundational advice for plant magic. And then, one of my favourite areas: edible plants and flowers. The idea that a lot of flowers are edible will open up a whole new area of magic for you, as well as being delicious, which gives a win-win situation. And that is just the beginning, as Patricia leads us into the realms of flower teas, wines, tantalising beverages, and culinary delights.

Not forgetting, of course, the amazing floral crafts that are included—it was this book that introduced me to flower petal beads—such a genius idea to create some magic that you can wear. And did I mention the floromancy and botanomancy? If you have not tried divination with flora and fauna, you don't know what you are missing. *A Floral Grimoire* gives you step-by-step instructions on how to work with this fascinating area of magic along with different variations of the practice.

There are, of course, a whole host of spells and charms using flowers, spices, and herbs too, drawing on ancient and historic folk magic. Simple but incredibly effective workings that anyone can use, that have the power of nature behind them.

This book is a *must-have* on any Witchcraft shelf and will open you up to a whole world of undiscovered floral magic.

Rachel Patterson

Introduction

*"To see the world in a grain of sand,
and heaven in a wildflower."*
—WILLIAM BLAKE

Nature's language is diverse, rich, and filled to overflowing with magic. Every tree, flower, leaf, and root represents one part of life's network and the creative force behind it. Our ancestors recognized this truth. They also saw the amazing inherent potential in nature's gifts, both temporal and spiritual, and then put that potential to good use every day.

Looking to the Victorians as an excellent example of ardent flower fanatics, blossoms could be found in everything from toiletries and decorations to the dinner table and the healer's kit. During this period, lovers developed an entire petaled vocabulary so that messages could be exchanged secretly. This vocabulary was steeped in the lore and superstitions associated with plants: superstitions that neatly hid magical beliefs beneath charming phrases and quaint actions. For example, herbs might be hung in a home or chapel, carried in a pocket, or presented to a child for luck and protection; and teatime on Sunday might be followed by a session of tea leaf readings amid a garden surrounding.

Victorians were certainly not the first to exhibit this kind of enthusiasm toward flowers and plants. One only has to look back to the Arabic spice traders during the Crusades for another example: cunning merchants often mingled magical lore and wives' tales into their selling techniques. This increased the value of their trade goods (mostly spices) and spread the metaphysical correspondences for herbs and flowers around the known world. During the Crusades and even Victorian times, it would not be unusual to find someone littering the floor of a room with rose petals to encourage love or hanging some garlic to keep wandering spirits away!

This zealous and somewhat playful attitude toward nature is something *A Floral Grimoire* seeks to emulate. The Earth's gifts to us are many. Each bit of flora can help us meet a variety of needs in powerful, life-affirming, and personally meaningful ways. In truth, I suspect that there isn't a plant on this planet that hasn't been used at least once, if not twice, for magic.

To begin, *A Floral Grimoire* peeks at how certain types of flora became associated with the occult arts and Witchery. Building on that premise, we'll also explore what's often called "green magic." This particular metaphysical school advocates honoring the Earth in our spiritual pursuits and explains the methods and mediums that have proven effective in supporting those pursuits.

That's not all! Have you ever wanted to create your own magical garden? The information shared here shows you how—even in an apartment! For that matter, did you know that a lot of flowers you might choose to cultivate are edible? *A Floral Grimoire* provides a hearty list of edible petals and sample recipes so that you can sow, harvest, and internalize your magical energy! Vegetarians will find that flowers represent a vitamin-filled, spiritually sustaining medium for their diets. And for those of you who don't fancy flower nibbling, I've provided help and hints for making your own goal-appropriate incense, candles, anointing oils, air fresheners, creams, and potpourri using nature's gifts.

Ascribing symbolic value to the natural world is a very ancient practice. With this in mind, *A Floral Grimoire* contains a section that describes easy ways to make your own divination tools based on that symbolism. In a highly technological society where we have fewer and fewer opportunities to really touch the Earth, these tools represent one way to commune with nature and listen to her voice on an intimate level no matter where you live. Better still, thanks to nature's diversity, you have a lot of plants to choose from for both the medium and emblems for your system!

It is but a short step from reading nature's language and symbols to learning how to cast spells, concoct charms, and create rituals with plants as important components and constructs. No book on flower and plant magic would be complete without a section that digs up the roots of this ancient art and shows you how to adapt and apply it today. With that in mind, I've supplied you with a plethora of hands-on magical methods that you can try or modify for all kinds of common needs.

Rounding everything out, there are easy instructions for various handcrafts that suit flowers and plants and ones that, when creatively applied, can augment your magic.

In whatever way you do it, I think you'll find that working with flowers and plants is very relaxing and satisfying. The more intimately involved you become in Green Witchery, the more you'll discover that nature has ways of speaking to our hearts about the things we most need to hear. She is a very gentle and helpful messenger. May this information help you in hearing that voice, and in rediscovering the magical power and potential that's been right under your feet all along: Earth!

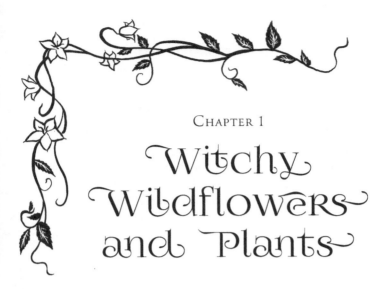

CHAPTER 1

Witchy Wildflowers and Plants

"What a desolate place would be a world without flowers? It would be a face without a smile; a feat without a welcome. Are not flowers the stars of earth? Are not our stars the flowers of heaven?"
—CLARA LOUISE BALFOUR

Greek myth tells us that Hecate, the patroness of Witches, instructed her daughters in the herbal arts. They, in turn, taught all Witches how to use this knowledge. Plant lore from that point forward became a sacred trust for wise people and cunning folk everywhere—for healing, love, fertility, prosperity, and most important to this material, for magic!

This myth, which is but one of many linking Witches and nature together, gives us a peek into the minds of our ancestors. It seems that our predecessors were a very superstitious lot. Exactly when and where all the superstitions about Witches and plants developed is fuzzy because it predates written history. What is quite certain is that historians, philosophers, and modern Witches alike have found it difficult, if not impossible, to read anything about one of these subjects without stumbling across information on the other.

For example, in reading a Celtic book about trees, you might discover that ash wood was essential in a Witch's broom to prevent drowning (you know how Witches hate water). In a medieval treatise on herbalism, you might discover that all Witches had to grow hemlock in their garden to honor Hecate...not to mention the herbs used in their wicked spells! According to these two guidelines, I would be considered only half-Witch, for I love to swim (no ash required) and the only hemlock in my garden is in the mulch!

Speaking of gardens, popular folklore has it that the sun should not be allowed to shine on a Witch's plants because the light would steal the power of the herbs. Around the magical garden, one could always find a hawthorn hedge to protect the power contained therein and provide the Witch with a handy place to hide. And what the Witch didn't grow themself, they'd find elsewhere. For example, if a broom wasn't handy, a Witch could gather a handful of hay to fly upon instead. While out and about, the Witch might also get some mullein to make candles and a harebell to use for a thimble.

Be that as it may, for every Witch-friendly herb in folklore, there is also an anti-Witch herb to keep us on our spiritual toes! These flowers and plants were just waiting to be plucked and carried, bound in sachets, sprinkled in wine, buried at a crossroad, or tossed into running water by someone who thought they were enchanted. One example is elderberry. When steeped in water and dabbed on a person's eyes, it allows that person to see a Witch no matter their guise. Another example is the combination of rowan and red thread, one of the most popular and powerful anti-magic charms.

Different cultures had their own unique outlook on Witchy wildflowers and plants. People in medieval Germany carried marjoram sprigs to safeguard themselves from a spell, but Witches in medieval France used them in love potions. Agrimony and hazel were used by Witch hunters to uncover occult activity, while the Witches themselves were using these plants to keep nasty critters like goblins at bay and to divine for water. Similarly, it was common practice (and still is in some areas) throughout Europe to lay a broom across the threshold to keep a Witch from entering, yet this very same broom could be used as the Witch's magical transportation.

In retrospect, all this superstition is rather amusing to a modern-minded Witch who has grown accustomed to logic and convenience. Even so, we have to consider the times and settings in which our ancestors lived—the beliefs they held dear were not just happenstance or whimsy. They had grown out of a long-term love affair that humankind developed with nature and her citizens. Through a combination of respect, faith, and old-fashioned "stick-to-it-iveness," the ancient magicians and cunning folk built a metaphysical system that would endure through the millennia to heal our bodies, nurture our minds, and advance our spirits.

Thus, superstitions about magical flowers and plants are actually very important to our studies and applications today. Underneath the leafy layers of lore are some notable historical roots and extremely useful correspondences that shouldn't be tossed away just because they're quaint by our standards. It is into these old roots that this information gently digs so that we can transplant the treasures found there into modern practice.

Rooting Around

The human fascination with flowers and plants dates back to antiquity, but its long-reaching effects on humanity are still being felt today. In both the metaphysical community and the public at large, the interest in natural medicine, non-chemical gardening methods, flowers as a food group, home herbalism, and other related fields has been growing steadily over the last few decades. Superficially, one might say that this has nothing to do with magic or Witches. Yet, since the village wise person, shaman, and Witch of old was often given the task of remembering and passing along our herbal heritage and traditional plant lore, it certainly does, as this is how we have our naturopathic information of today.

In reviewing the brief history that follows here, please bear in mind that these people truly trusted in magic as a means to improve their life—something we would do well to emulate.

The Original Spiritual Botanists

Flower and plant magic has been utilized effectively by wives, warriors, charlatans, shamans, and dreamers of all ages. It is important to remember, however, that we are exploring documentable history here versus oral tradition. Oral history indicates that the fascination humanity has had for the natural world began almost as soon as the mind could comprehend a "tomorrow." Written history doesn't take us quite that far back.

The oldest written records of plant lore come to us from Egypt. Here, the idea of medicine, perfumery, and magic were united into a "metaphysical" system of cures and allures. The earliest papyruses containing plant lore date from 2000 to 1000 BC but refer frequently to older texts and oral traditions. These writings talk about the use of various plants in embalming, one of the most important religious traditions for Egyptians. From these, evidence suggests that the Hanging Gardens of Babylon likely housed flowers, herbs, and other plants for all types of practical, religious, and magical functions.

Similarly, in India, plant lore and religion mingled freely in a system known as *Ayurveda* (1500 BC), which meant "the science of life." It was believed that the gods originally taught Ayurveda to a handful of human disciples. These faithful few placed this information in the Vedas (Hindu scriptures) for the edification of the general populace. By 1000 BC, these techniques were highly developed and expanded in the Rigveda, where over 1,000 plants were listed. This was followed in AD 1, by *Charaka Sambita*, a text listing 500 herbal drugs alongside strong recommendations for people to include meditation in their daily routine as a way of building a healthy body-mind-spirit balance.

Moving from India into the Graeco-Roman world, around the seventh century BC, we find the Greeks still observing nature's magic with awe and respect, as did the Syrians, Mesopotamians, and Persians (to name just a few). In large trade-oriented regions such as Greece and Rome, magical plant lore was absorbed by all types of travelers, from merchants to kings. During this period, we also find some Witches and magicians working quietly in villages, while others assist rulers.

By the early centuries AD, trouble was starting to brew between the Pagan and Christian factions over retaining a social versus theological worldview. Nonetheless, natural magic and Church ritual still mingled pretty liberally at this point, most likely fueled by respected Greek philosopher Aristotle's declaration that plants possessed a powerful psyche, albeit less than that of humans. The secret powers of herbs and plants were being used readily to heal, divine the future, make amulets, and so forth. In some instances, this very Pagan tradition included a mingling of Christian invocations just for good measure.

Sometime between AD 100 and AD 500, the Gnostic and Hermetic traditions began to mingle. This resulted in long incantations that exhibited the blend of Jewish, Christian, Hellenistic, Persian, Greek, and Babylonian influences. Alongside this, we find still more attention to the natural world and its magic. Specifically, in the early herbal writings of *Hermetica* (a book sometimes historically attributed to Hermes Trismegistus, a syncretization of the Greek god Hermes and the Egyptian god Thoth) we find plants categorized by their planetary, divine, and sympathetic associations. For example, any herb linked with Venus (the planet) was also often associated with the goddess, meaning that the flower or herb would be powerful in love magic! Sound familiar? It should, since modern Witches still sort out flowers and plants in this manner.

During this same time, Cassiodorus, a Roman senator and monk (490–58 BC), created a monk's curriculum complete with herbal studies. These herbal curatives included all manner of charms, incantations (with Pagan god or goddess names changed to suitable divine or angelic names), and mystical properties. While no monk would ever think of himself as studying the occult, these men were expected to perform duties from healing the sick to making both fields and livestock fertile. Such rites continued well into the twelfth century, supported by various books on "leeching" (healing with herbs complete with instructions, verbal charms, taboos, and ritualistic overtones) and the common people's mingling of Pagan and Christian ways. Even up to one hundred years ago, books were rare and costly and had to serve several functions, so the typical health book of the day was often a kind of catch-all, including crop, household, and other information.

We move next into the Graeco-Arabic tradition. Between AD 641 and AD 1096, monasteries were often the centers where plant lore and herbal arts were dutifully tended. Cunning folk were also common during this time, being trusted by the townspeople, they served for everything from curing cattle to easing the pain of a broken heart. These cunning folk were truly wise in that they blended pragmatic know-how (often having learned their art at the feet of a mentor, master, or parent) with metaphysical energy. The result was a potent balance between temporal and spiritual, mundane and magical. This is an example well worth following today.

Meanwhile, across the seas in Japan, we find still more evidence of the global reverence toward flowers, specifically chrysanthemums. On the ninth day of the ninth moon, petals were steeped in wine and given to the emperor to ensure long life and inspire the muse. This was also the day when the shogun met with his samurai as a show of fealty. It's interesting to note that this very ancient celebration continues in modern times with flower shows in early September to honor Japanese history and tradition.

Also during this time, the Arabic people were busy developing the profession of pharmacist (c. AD 900). This job wasn't simply a matter of prescriptions. These pharmacists were well-studied physicians who employed astrology and various "magically" related rituals as part of their healing techniques, especially that of preparing medicines. After the Crusades (1096–1271), Arabic beliefs were brought back to Europe and added to the wealth of herbal treatments already applied.

When the clever Arab spice traders met the Europeans, they quickly recognized a lucrative atmosphere full of magic, omens, and Witchcraft, ripe for harvesting. They used this foundation as an advertising platform, spreading traditional Arabic plant lore associated with their spices and raising the value of their trade goods in the process. So talented were their efforts that the Muslim hold on the spice trade did not diminish for centuries.

Apart from the Arabic practices, the common people of this time employed the renowned magical significance of herbs for boon and bane as needed. Parsley was taken to prevent drunkenness, anise for nightmares, basil for hatred, and laurel was taken to invoke the gift of prophesy. This is the rich stock from which evolved many of our modern plant correspondences.

At the start of the second millennium, the continuous mingling of magic with more scientific approaches for using flowers and plants makes it difficult to sort out one from the other. The common person likely chose whatever process and plant part was known to be effective, and whatever was readily available, along with utilizing special timing to obtain the desired results. For example, petals might be gathered at dawn or when the moon was waxing to symbolically encourage energy to "grow." Witches today still follow this tradition when their schedules allow.

During the 1200s, there appeared a book entitled *Lacnunga*, whose author is unknown. It was an important compilation of prescriptions from European folk magic, including bits from Anglo-Saxon, Celtic, and Norse traditions that helped document many commonly used healing methods. It also described the flowers and plants called for in various spells, potions, and amulets along with suitable accompanying incantations and ritualistic preparation processes.

What's particularly interesting to the modern practitioner is the fact that the construct of incantations, the use of color and number symbolism, and the application of astrology all sound very much like what we read in magical texts today.

Additionally, during these years, the word *occult* was used more as we wish it were used today—to indicate a kind of specialized, semi-scientific study of nature in an effort to uncover the greater mysteries. No doubt, we can thank alchemists for this positive influence. Unfortunately, some members of this group also brought an air of secrecy to magic, feeling that flower and plant powers were best learned orally, from teacher to select student, and should not be readily available to the public.

During the 1300s, the herbal tradition continued with other topical tomes. Some told of how notable figures like St. Augustine used plants and plant parts as spiritual helpmates. Solomon's herb, for example, was used by the saint to exorcise evil. This herb was not to be taken internally as a curative, but instead, hung around the neck and shown to the afflicted person so any nearby demons would fly away! This is a perfect description of what Witches call a *talisman* or *fetish* (a specially chosen object with inherent power that evokes some type of immediate response), yet it was used by a Christian saint. In this manner, St. Augustine quite innocently helped salvage the tradition of natural magic from the grips of disappearing history and increasing social transition.

In the early 1400s, we discover an interesting woman in Todi, Italy, known as Matteuccia Francisci. This woman was truly a professional Witch and could often be found mixing over thirty plant parts into wine for love, fertility, or other curatives. She also created lotions and poppets for similar purposes. Apparently, Matteuccia's abilities, knowledge of plant lore, and adeptness with the magical arts were substantial enough that she had clients who traveled to see her from far away.

By the next century in England, well-known herbalists were proving themselves almost as spicy as their subject matter. John Gerard, an herbalist in the sixteenth century, first published his herbal work in 1597, which actually was a rewrite of Rembert Dodoens' *Cruydeboeck* in part! To his credit, Gerard also included information on exotic plants, of which he personally grew over 1,000 species, and added the rich flora, fauna, and associated plant lore of England.

He was followed in the mid-1600s by Nicholas Culpeper, an herbalist and astrologer who listed planetary associations in his writings, and whether a plant was "hot" or "cold" (which affected its applications). Alongside Culpeper, the German alchemist Albertus Magnus's (c. 1193–1280) work entitled *The Boke of Secrets* had become very popular by this time (originally appearing in the 1500s). Magnus taught Thomas Aquinas alchemy, and his writings include information on the mystical virtues of herbs, flowers (like periwinkle, lily, and rose), and plants like mistletoe.

Exactly why it took so long for Magnus's work to become public is uncertain. Some historians think that an anonymous writer may have actually "borrowed" Magnus's name for recognition. Nonetheless, the value of this book is unquestioned; writers and students of both magic and herbalism have studied and quoted it ever since.

The seventeenth century finds some rather famous people ascribing to the magic of flowers and plants, so it's not surprising that everyday people followed their lead. King Louis XIV's mistress, for example (mid- to late-1600s) employed a popular Witch, Catherine la Voisin, to create love potions, passion mixtures, and beauty preparations. In these preparations, we find common flowers still used today for love (like roses), and culinary spices like fennel, cinnamon, and nutmeg because they were readily available and had the right energies. This is also a good example to follow in our flower and plant magic; as long as we maintain congruency of meaning, we can use whatever we have on hand for our efforts. By the 1700s, the demand for magicians still existed, but humans as a whole were undergoing a kind of mental awakening to the wonders of science. Alchemy became more appealing because of its scientific methods, even to figures like Johann Wolfgang von Goethe. Nonetheless, we don't read too much of Witchery during this time, most likely due to the remaining sting of the Witch hunts in Europe and America. Instead, Freemasonry, which has mystical overtones, makes a strong appearance along with some Druidry, which brings us back to nature's temple.

A strong interest in the occult arts appeared once more in the nineteenth century. Cabalism, agnosticism, heretics, alchemy, and Pythagoreanism all found themselves experiencing a renaissance. Books on these subjects started to appear, filled with useful plant lore. Éliphas Lévi, a mystic from the 1800s and revered as the "father of modern magic," wrote during this era for ritual magicians, while other people were compiling magical almanacs for everyday folks, not simply researchers or historians. While illiteracy was still common, this period marks an important transition for those interested in magic. It was no longer going to be an exclusive club, and it has remained open to anyone who wanted to know about it ever since.

It's also important to notice that no matter the era or culture examined in this brief review, the magical arts have always worked hand in hand with the natural world, and still do. In a wide variety of methods and traditions, herbs, flowers, and other plants were key constituents for cunning folk. This means we have a vast global heritage from which to draw upon today. By doing so, we can benefit from our ancestors' experiences and honor our history, while still being mindful of the times in which we live and the flower and plant data now available.

Flowers of the Gods, Heroes, and Immortals

In looking at the world's natural history, and how that history affects humans, it's impossible not to stumble across many interesting stories of gods, goddesses, and other important historical or mythical figures. Some of these divine beings shared their names and were otherwise associated with various sacred flowers and plants. Other gods and goddesses cared for the natural kingdom, and still others appeared like parts of nature at whim!

This is probably why flower and tree names are so often linked with gods and goddesses of many cultures, and why many deities received offerings of nature. Aphrodite (Greece) and Venus (Rome), for example, received myrtle as an offering.

Venus's alternative name in some parts of Rome was Myrtilla for this reason. Roses were also sacred to these two love goddesses, some myths saying that roses actually sprouted from Venus's bathwater.

Offerings weren't the only reason that flowers and plants were gathered to honor Divine beings. At various celebrations, flower petals and other plant parts littered the temples and parade routes. For Apollo, bay leaves and heliotrope were predominant. Minerva received olive branches, Mars was given ash spears or poles, Bacchanalia included ivy and grapes (of course), and statues of Ceres might be adorned with poppies during her feast days.

Some flowers and plants got their names from various gods and goddesses who were known to meddle in human affairs. Mint, for example, received its name from a maiden, Minthe, who was being pursued by Pluto. Persephone, being a jealous sort, turned the maiden into the mint plant. It is, after all, a little difficult to get romantic with a leafy herb!

And, if that's not bad enough, it seems many mortals were doomed to being turned into plants due to divine wrath, as a way of compensating for some divine wrong-doing, or to protect them from unwanted godly attention! Violets, for example, were created by Cupid from a group of young maidens whom Venus beat during a jealous rage. This was one way Cupid could restore the women's beauty. The violet remains a sacred flower to Cupid.

Despite their somewhat human failings, the gods and goddesses also seemed to give attributes to various flowers and plants, even unintentionally. Geraniums, for example, sprang from the sweat of Muhammad, and lilies grew from Eve's tears when she was expelled from Eden. Christian legend says that lavender flowers had no aroma until Mary dried Jesus' clothing on a lavender plant. Similarly, the rose bore no color until a drop of Aphrodite's blood touched it and it had no thorns until a young Cupid was stung by a bee while admiring the flower. His goddess mother simply transferred the thorny stings to the plant's stem. Presumably, the rose also had no scent until Cupid upset a cup of nectar near it and saturated it with a sweet aroma. My, can you imagine a white, scentless, un-thorned rose?

While most of the stories I've shared here originate in Graeco-Roman tradition, they are not unique in global myth. For example, the Hindu god of love, Kama, has a bow with five arrows, each of which is topped with a flower. When a human is struck with this petal power, it overwhelms that person, and they fall madly in love! In the Eastern part of the world, one of the ancient names for the goddess Padma means "lotus," and many Hindu gods and goddesses are thought to be "lotus-born," indicating the flower's importance.

In ancient Persian tradition, the goddess Ameretat presided over the plant kingdom, and the god Haoma was lord over healing plants and those that confer immortality. (It's notable that Haoma is also the name of a specific plant used in religious worship in present-day Iran.)

Egyptians had the plant god Uneg, while ancient Aztecs had the flower prince Xochipilli, who also ruled over games and the hours of the day (this would make a great deity to call on to bless a clock garden—one in which plants open at specific hours so you can tell the time by them). In Baltic traditions, Zemyna is the mother of plants who is invoked with the words "she who raises flowers." Pre-Columbian Peru had Chasca Coyllur, the god of flowers, who protected young maidens. In Tibet, the demigods, called *Vidyadhara*, possess the knowledge of using the supernatural powers of plants. These beings often bore garlands of flowers as they flew on the winds.

The Chinese immortal known as Han Xiangzi could make flowers grow and bloom at will (it's not surprising this character is often depicted with a basket of flowers). Another illustration from China is the lore surrounding chrysanthemums. In China, America, and elsewhere, chrysanthemum petals are believed to endow vitality and long life because of a myth about immortality. A Japanese legend tells of Kikujido, a Chinese boy who fled to the Valley of Chrysanthemums to avoid the emperor's wrath. He was thirsty and gathered dew from chrysanthemum petals to drink, which gave him eternal life.

From these tales, and others like them, it's easy to see that the lives of mortals, heroes, and gods have often been influenced in some way by flowers and plants. At first glance, these stories may not seem all that relevant to our study, but, since many magical practitioners choose to call on one or several gods or goddesses to bless and energize their spells and rituals, knowing which ones rule over specific plants and flowers is very helpful in designing magical methods.

How? Well, let's look to the lily for an example. Lilies are sacred to Venus, Juno, and Kwan Yin. So, individuals working with lilies in a specific spell or charm might call upon one of these goddesses as part of an invocation to empower the charm. Or, someone with one of these goddesses as a patroness might adorn her altar with lilies, burn lily incense, or bathe in lily-scented water beforehand to honor her.

While it is not necessary to involve the gods in metaphysical methods unless you so choose, it is an idea worth keeping in mind as you read the rest of this material. When you feel you'd like a little extra universal energy to give your natural magic a nudge, the deities can certainly help. Besides acting as a manifesting force, they can guide the magic safely to its mark, so it truly works for the "greatest good."

In meditation or dreamwork, the deity who presides over specific plants can teach you about effectively using those items in your magic. From a devotional standpoint, it pleases your patron or patroness when you take the time to learn about (and use) the magical flowers, herbs, and plants that are sacred to them. Finally, if the plants and flowers associated with your personal god or goddess keep appearing in your life, knowing with whom they're associated could provide you with an important clue to a divine message.

My only caution in working with gods and goddesses is this: Make sure you respectfully educate yourself about the being upon whom you call (such as how to pronounce their name) and honor them appropriately in your sacred space. Just as you would not randomly open your door to a stranger and ask for their help, the deities upon whom you call should be those with whom you've developed a special rapport, be it from your path, your culture, your personal experiences, or from your family. This will make your connections with them much more meaningful and spiritually fulfilling.

Flower Fancy

Earlier in this material, I discussed a bit of plant and flower lore that was (and often still is) associated with Witchery. Since my goal is for you to become more familiar with various superstitions and lore and use them effectively in modern magic, I want to spend some time discussing a few "how-to" methods of the Craft.

Let's begin with some anti-magic and anti-Witch herbs. Now, I know some of you must be wondering why on earth one would want to know about the plants and flowers that were considered *anti-magic* agents. The reason is that many of these plants *were* and *are still* used metaphysically for other purposes. So, if you use one in a spell or ritual and things seem to go askew, it might be because the plant's overall energy is best suited to anti-magic. It simply did its job! Give something else a try!

Here is a sampling of some anti-magic and anti-Witch herbs, flowers, and plants:

ALYSSUM: Protects the bearer from charm and fascination.

ANGELICA: Cures bewitchment and curses or deflects them from you.

ANISE: A sure-fire ward against the evil eye.

ASH: Protection against sorcery and conjury.

BAMBOO: Used for hex-breaking and banishing.

BASIL: This purges an area of magical influences.

BEANS (ANY DRIED KIND): Turns away magically generated misfortune.

BROOM: Hung in the home or placed across the doorway, this will turn back Witches.

CHAMOMILE: Averts any kind of spell.

CHRYSANTHEMUM: Protects the home against evoked spirits and averts magical mayhem.

CINQUEFOIL: Washes away hexes.

CORIANDER: Protective herb that fights off mystical evils.

DILL: Protects the bearer from Witchery when carried over the heart.

ELDER: Used to identify whether or not a person is a real Witch.

FENNEL: Hung in the doorway on a midsummer's day, it will turn away any mal-intended magic.

GARLIC: A good all-around preventative against magical creatures and unwanted spells.

HOLLY: Protection against the evil eye, no matter how powerful the caster.

HYACINTH: Cures fascination.

IVY (GROUND): When fashioned into a cross, this was thought helpful to Witch-hunters.

MALLOW: Fights off black magic.

MARJORAM: German Witches cannot tolerate this herb.

MISTLETOE: Carry this to avert evil spells.

NETTLE: Dispels magical curses.

OATS: Protects horses and other animals from curses, especially the evil eye.

ROWAN: Bound with red thread, it becomes a powerful anti-magic charm.

SAGE: Protects against curses cast with a wicked glance.

ST. JOHN'S WORT: Forces a Witch to confess the truth.

VALERIAN: Hung in the home, it protects all within from malevolent magic.

VERVAIN: When combined with dill, this makes a very potent anti-Witchcraft amulet.

WALNUT: If you put this under a true Witch's seat, they will be unable to move.

In reading this list, one might be inclined to think that everyone feared magic and Witches, and that nearly every Witch must be up to no good! Ah, but that's not so. We need to bear in mind that the times in which our ancestors lived were simpler than ours, and so often lacked explanation for things that frightened, confused, or astounded people. In response to this, protective lore against "magic" developed. Besides, any modern Witch will happily tell you that we're only mischievous *part* of the time.

More seriously, for every superstition aimed at banishing Pagan influences, there were others that augmented or honored those influences, even if somewhat indirectly. Here are some examples:

AGRIMONY: Reverses spells placed upon a mage.

ANISE: An overall magical helpmate, especially to protect a high magician from angry, invoked spirits.

BIRCH: The traditional wood for a Witch's broom handle.

CATNIP: Excellent to help Witches improve their rapport with cat familiars.

CELERY SEED: This was once thought to help Witches fly.

CHAMOMILE: An indispensable herb for the green-thumbed Witch; this energizes the whole garden with magic.

CLOVE: Improves overall magical energy.

CORIANDER: A powerful herb spirit that energizes magical gardens.

CYPRESS: Increases the power of a Witch's invocations.

DRAGON'S BLOOD: Increases overall magic power.

ECHINACEA: Used to invoke spirits to help with magical workings.

ELDER: Can house a Witch's spirit.

EYEBRIGHT: Improves a magician's psychic powers.

FIG: A natural charming agent.

GARDENIA: Increases positive vibrations for Witchcraft.

GERANIUM: Warns Witches of approaching guests, especially strangers.

GINGER: A power-enhancing herb.

HAWTHORN: Witches can turn themselves into this tree for protection.

HEMLOCK: This helps the Witch travel astrally.

JUNIPER: Carry this to improve magical and spiritual awareness.

LEMON: The Witch's alternative to a poppet in sympathetic magic.

MUGWORT: Improves psychic awareness.

MULBERRY: Used by Witches to safeguard spell books.

MYRRH: Acts as a magical blessing and clears the sacred space of unwanted energies before a ritual or spell.

PERIWINKLE: The folk name of Sorcerer's violet says a lot. This is an overall pro-magic herb, especially useful for Witchery.

POPLAR: A tree used for water Witching (as a divining rod) indicating its inherent magical power for aiding a Witch with fortune-telling.

VALERIAN: Used to improve a Witch's rapport with spirits.

WILLOW: Used to bind a Witch's broom.

As we move from this whimsical review to the rest of this information, you'll quickly see that very specific flowers and herbs were used for equally specific magical functions. These associations arose out of folk traditions, myths, our ancestors' clever ideas and observations, and especially out of the tradition of Green Witchcraft. The Witch knows that Earth is a friend and nature is generous. As long as we treat them in kind, the magical lore of plants and flowers will always serve us well.

CHAPTER 2

Green Magic

*"If you wish to know the divine, feel the wind on
your face and the warm sun on your hand."*
—BUDDHA

A Native American by the name of Rolling Thunder once said that the "Great Spirit is the life that is in all things." People who practice green magic recognize this truth and find themselves captivated by the divine pattern of power imprinted on every blade, leaf, and blossom. This fascination engages the Green Witch's soul to the point where they rediscover a deep abiding respect for the wonders of creation and then live accordingly. Most importantly, the Green Witch reflects natural awareness and appreciation by the way they undertake all magical methods.

Since one of the purposes of this material is to help you practice effective Green Witchery, these pages represent an important step along the path. Remember to take time out from your life's hectic pace to reevaluate your relationship to the world, and specifically to nature. Ask yourself how often you stop to appreciate the unique turn of a leaf just before it rains, to inhale the amazing aroma of freshly sprouted spring grass, or to revel in a late blossoming flower that stubbornly clings to life even as winter's threshold approaches. These gestures may seem very simple and small, but for a Green Witch, they're nothing less than essential. Such mindful actions and perspectives build a symbiotic awareness of, and relationship with, the flowers and plants you'll be using in your magic. Living in this manner is more spiritually and personally fulfilling because it begins to open your mind to seeing the magical potential in everything.

Once you begin seeing the entire Earth this way, both you and your magic will change forever. Where some people are forever seeking spiritual flash and fanfare, the Green Witch celebrates the wondrous, unadorned magic that's right under our noses all the time. From this perspective, nothing is too simple or plain to function effectively in our magical efforts.

Better still, Green Witchery inspires a lot of spontaneous spells and charms and gives us some fun ways to recycle. Say, for example, that you're walking along and a leaf falls at your feet. Most people would just keep walking. Not the clever Green Witch! They see the leaf as a gift or message from nature's spirit, and will certainly put that gift to good use in any number of ways, like:

- Seeing what kind of tree it came from to determine if the leaf is some kind of omen or sign.
- Drying the leaf and adding it to a suitably themed magical incense.
- Carrying the leaf (especially if it's oak) as an amulet against sickness.
- Whispering a wish to the leaf and releasing it back to the winds for manifestation.
- Burning the leaf in a fire and observing the flames to help answer a pressing question (a form of pyromancy).
- Floating the leaf on a puddle while thinking of a question and observing the movements for a symbolic response.
- Tossing the leaf in a swift-flowing stream so as to carry a problem or sickness away.
- Waxing the leaf and putting it in a special magical book to bring beauty to that page.

From this brief list, you can see that Green Witchery puts forward a whole world of possibilities for your magical arts and crafts: The world of nature. It also provides you with a peek into the Green Witch's worldview. In brief, a Green Witch is one who:

- Recognizes that humans do not have dominion over the Earth. Rather, we are partners with the Earth.
- Experiences the Earth as intimately as possible.
- Protects natural resources as circumstances will allow.
- Reunites themself with Earth energies and Gaia's spirit.
- Uses flowers and plants as components in spellcraft or as a focus for other magical methods.
- Motivates greater Earth awareness in others.
- Lives beyond the normal boundaries we place on ourselves, seeing no absolute divisions in life's network. The distance between you and a flower is but a thought.

Finally, and perhaps most importantly, the Green Witch knows that it is truly sacred ground on which we walk (even when it's hidden underneath the pavement). Earth is there, just waiting for Green Witches everywhere to reclaim the magic!

Communing with Plant Spirits

Far more than being a simple gathering of roots, stems, and leaves, Green Witches regard flowers and plants as having spirits all their own. In some schools of thought, these spirits are the deva (pronounced *day-va*), the fairy folk, who tend to nature's needs and reflect the dynamics of the Earth's elements (Earth-Air-Fire-Water). In other belief systems, like shamanism, the plants themselves have an astral presence and personality with which one can communicate. Now, I know it's really hard to imagine yourself suddenly talking to the neighbor's shrubs to get magical advice, or asking the shrubs why they aren't growing well! Nonetheless, those are exactly what a Green Witch can do once they have developed a rapport with plant spirits. In pondering this aspect of Green Witchery, I am reminded of a quote by E. P. Whipple, a nineteenth-century essayist, that says it all: "The apple that she (nature) drops at Newton's feet is but a coy invitation to follow her to the stars." Nature's spirits really do offer us that invitation, and so much more.

What benefit does communing with plant spirits offer the spiritual seeker? First, the spirits can tell us about how to heal the land and reclaim it. This is especially important with the amount of pollution and deforestation that is affecting every corner of our planet. They can guide us in fighting specific types of pests, or in supporting plant species that are in danger of extinction. Perhaps most important to this material, plant spirits become helpers in our quest to know when to sow, harvest, and prepare our magical flora, and what greenery is best for the metaphysical process or theme we have planned.

No matter what any book says about a specific plant's magical correspondence, those authors weren't around to witness that plant's growth or environment. Every plant has slightly different growing conditions (water, sunlight, soil quality, etc.) that can (and will) change the mystical properties of that plant. What better way to give us insights into this life cycle and its transformative effect than the plant itself!

To illustrate, say a bay plant experiences an unusually wet season. Bay is normally associated with the element of Fire. It's used magically to produce prophetic dreams (placed under a pillow), and as an herb that generates physical strength when worn as a charm. When you commune with this particular plant's spirit, however, you discover that the leaves will produce dreams more readily when steeped as in tea, or provide emotional strength when carried because of the water element's influence on that plant's basic matrix. So, when we know how to look and listen, plant spirits provide very valuable insights. All in all, Mother Earth truly does know best!

Spiritual Eyes and Ears

Having said all that, just how do you go about getting in touch with a plant spirit? In reviewing various magical traditions, there seems to be a pattern that repeats. The methods that appear most frequently are presented here for your consideration, with but one precaution:

Don't just jump in and try anything unless it really makes sense to you, and unless you plan to take the effort very seriously.

Any shaman will tell you that if you insult a plant spirit, you will never be able to work effectively with that plant again, so you'll want to get it right the first time!

1. If possible, grow the plant yourself. This will give you direct physical contact with it regularly before attempting spiritual contact.

2. If the plant is edible, add it to your diet regularly for an entire week before trying to make contact. This internalizes the plant's energy and creates an inner harmony with that plant's matrix, which will ultimately improve your results.

3. Sensually experience the plant. Touch it, smell it, listen to the sound it makes in the wind or rain, and look at it from different angles (above, below, and from all sides). Again, I suggest doing this daily for a full week before you attempt to make contact.

4. Bring the plant into your life in as many ways as possible, like wearing its pattern on a tie or shirt, hanging a picture of it near your desk, burning incense in its aroma, and so forth.

5.   When you feel ready, meditate with the plant nearby. Try to make sure you won't be disturbed for at least twenty minutes.

6.   As you meditate, breathe deeply and wait until you feel "transported," maybe a little fuzzy around the edges of your being (some people describe this as tingling, or hearing a far-off humming sound).

7.   Now, visualize yourself in an environment in which that plant would naturally grow. See yourself sitting in the middle of a circle of these flowers or plants. Allow this visualization to become as real as possible, bringing to memory the smell of the plant, its texture, and everything else you learned about it in the previous steps.

8.   Reach out spiritually toward the plant. Don't open your physical eyes, open your psychic ones. Be patient and wait, making mental notes of any imagery or feelings from this point forward.

Plant spirits will generally communicate empathically, or through one of your senses. This type of communication is much easier for our minds to accept and interpret (after all, the idea of a sunflower suddenly talking to you is a bit much for most modern folk to handle). So, pay attention to how you feel, if the air changes somehow, if the imagery around you shifts, or if the plant moves, seems to grow, or suddenly blossoms. All these things are good indications that you've achieved contact.

From this point on, how the plant spirit communicates with you will be very personal and based on the questions you have in mind. Once rapport is established, let the spirit know the purpose of your visit quickly and respectfully. Try not to anticipate any particular response, as this could lead you to overlook important, subtle signals the spirit provides.

At some point, the spirit will withdraw, which means it's also time for you to return to normal levels of awareness. Let your breathing resume its previous rate, allowing the Earth to gather any excess energy like a magnet. Then, while the experience is still fresh in your mind, make notes or tape-record everything you recall. Study this information later when you use this particular flower or plant in your magical arts.

NOTE: The experience you have with one rosebush will likely be totally different from another rosebush, so don't assume it will be the same. Say, for example, that you've chosen to use a different rosebush in a spell because of its symbolic color value (yellow roses represent friendship, red ones reflect passion and love, and white ones are for peace). You should probably consider going through the whole communion process with a specific bush to be certain of your choice. It is a little time-consuming but yields the best results and the greatest amount of insight into the magical applications for any given plant.

Nature's Cycles

The Green Witch knows that nature provides us with many clues about when to plan our magical efforts so that they produce the best possible results. These clues come from the Moon, the Sun, and the seasons, and they direct us to certain conclusions about when to sow and reap our magical flowers and plants for the most potent energies. When Green Witches use these symbolic aspects of nature's cycles, it generates sympathetic support for the magic at hand.

MAGIC IN THE MOON

The Moon's cycles are, by far, the most utilized natural "cue" for magical practitioners. In the lunar sphere's waxing and waning, we find a great deal of symbolism that has been used by shamans and Witches alike for thousands of years. It was once even believed that Witches got their powers from the Moon, and for a Green Witch, there is some truth to this. The Moon's energy affects our flowers and plants, and their applications, so indirectly it also makes an impact on our art.

The way in which this information will affect your gardening (specifically sowing and weeding times) will be covered in future material. For the purpose of harvesting a magical plant or timing your use of greenery in a spell, ritual, or charm, however, you can refer to the list that follows here. Note that this is but a brief overview of the energy associated with various moon phases and moon signs. You can find more detailed information, and discover exactly when these phases and signs occur by referring to a magical almanac.

WAXING MOON: Suited to magical matters that require steady growth, even pacing, and positive development.

FULL MOON: The mystical themes of this phase are maturity, fertility, productivity, manifestation, and creativity.

WANING MOON: Time your spells or pick your herbs during a waning moon to banish negativity or decrease unwanted energies.

BLUE MOON: Blue moons are ideal for planning wish magic or anything that requires a metaphysical miracle.

MOON IN ARIES: Use this sign for overcoming obstacles and developing personal skills.

MOON IN TAURUS: A Taurus moon helps develop tenacity, and provides energy for abundance.

MOON IN GEMINI: A Gemini moon encourages balance and positive transformation.

MOON IN LEO: Leo's moon guides us in finding our "voice," especially in the magical arts.

MOON IN VIRGO: The Virgo moon provides supportive energy for prosperity and success.

MOON IN LIBRA: Libra's moon emphasizes balance. It also helps in uncovering mysteries or secrets.

MOON IN SCORPIO: Scorpio's moon is one of focus, especially on physical issues like the expression of passion.

MOON IN SAGITTARIUS: The Sagittarius moon builds self-control and helps manifest goals.

MOON IN CAPRICORN: Capricorn's moon makes you aware of the true you, and provides spiritual sustenance.

MOON IN AQUARIUS: The Aquarian moon develops an awareness of the simple beauties and potentials, which makes it very suited to Green Witchery. It also increases your energy for adventures.

MOON IN PISCES: The Pisces moon is one of abundance, movement, and improving your intuitive senses.

I ordinarily suggest that, if possible, you do your moon work outdoors in the moonlight. However, knowing that many readers live in cities where this may not be feasible, just knowing that the moon is there is enough. In a magical construct, your spiritual awareness of the lunar cycles is just as important to your success, or perhaps more so, than actually working in the moonlight.

THE SUNNY SIDE OF THE STREET

After reading all about the Moon, I'm sure some of you are wondering about the sky's other resident. In magic, the Sun represents the conscious mind, logic, rationality, leadership, strength, and the masculine aspect of the universe. So, you might harvest magical plants or plan your Green Witchery processes for daylight hours, when the goal of your magic matches solar symbolism. You can also consider each portion of the day as you might a moon phase, as follows:

DAWN: A time of transforming negatives, attracting hope, and inspiring renewal. If you're looking for a fresh start in any situation, this is an excellent time to work your magic.

EARLY MORNING: From a practical standpoint, this is a good time to harvest flowers before the heat of the day withers them or lessens their aroma. Spiritually, it's a good time to focus on gently increasing physical energy or improving mental keenness.

NOON: The Sun's most powerful time of the day. This is a good hour to direct your magic toward the element of Fire (working with Fire-aligned plants), shining a light on anything that needs a fresh perspective, and physical health.

DUSK: As the Sun sets, it creates a gentle balance between light and dark. Dusk is like a waning moon: it marks the types of endings that lead to new beginnings. So if you're planning to leave a job or relationship and want to make sure this is a wisely considered action, dusk is a good time to harvest your spell components or work your magic.

MIDNIGHT: Though you cannot see the Sun in the sky at this hour, it is shining somewhere in the world. Keep that in the back of your mind as you work your spells.

Midnight is the Witching hour, a time when the veil between worlds and dimensions grows thin. It's also a time that hovers on the edge of the old and the new day—it is both today and tomorrow. So, work your green magic at midnight when you want to build a better day, when you're planning astral travel, or to improve your rapport with spirits and devas.

SEASONS

The Wheel of the Year is also very important to the Green Witch because every season has very specific chores and equally specific magic that's suited to those months. While it's obvious that not every human need can be perfectly timed to slide into the yearly cycle, it helps to know what types of energy each season sustains. This way, even if you can't gather your plants or work your magic during a special moon sign or hour of the day, you can look to a whole season for options instead:

SPRING: The themes for this season are fertility, hope, inspiration, growth, and renewal. In particular, consider using new grass, tree blossoms, or an early budding flower in your green magic to represent the season of rebirth.

SUMMER: The themes for this season are prosperity, energy, health, abundance, socialization, and playfulness. In particular, consider using fresh sunflowers, daisies, and Fire-associated herbs like rosemary in your summertime green magic.

FALL: The themes for this season are in-gathering (manifestation), protection (especially health), frugality, and harvesting the fruits of your labors with thankfulness. In particular, consider using any traditional harvest plant in your magic (like apples or corn).

WINTER: The themes for this season are rest, home and family, tradition, and safeguarding your resources in both literal and figurative terms. In particular, consider using dried flowers and plant parts to honor the season, or perhaps berries to symbolize spring's forthcoming abundance.

For those readers who don't live in a four-season environment, carefully consider the symbolic value of any regular changes that occur around you. The rainy season, for example, might bear energies aligned with the Water element (intuition, emotion, psychism, lunar magic, etc.). A long snowy season might equate to having plants suited to slowing or halting specific types of energy (e. g., freezing it), and a dry season could equate to using those plants for fire magic.

By the way, even Green Witches who have four seasons should pay attention to shifts in local weather patterns. When weather varies dramatically from the norm throughout the season, this will affect the entire season's themes. For example, a very dry spring might yield plants suited to slow progress when things are moving too quickly (dryness slows down plant growth). Please keep these kinds of things in mind throughout this material, and whenever you practice green magic.

The Doctrine of Signatures and Magical Sympathy

The Doctrine of Signatures and the idea of Magical Sympathy are very old, time-honored systems used in Green Witchery. Knowing these two principles will also prove helpful in considering any type of metaphysical process.

Let's begin with the Doctrine of Signatures, popularized in the 1600s by Jakob Böhme, a German mystic. Many ancient people of notable status, like Paracelsus (a fifteenth- to sixteenth-century Swiss alchemist and physician) and Robert Turner (a seventeenth-century astrological botanist), treasured this doctrine and used it regularly both for experimentation and prescriptions. Essentially, the Doctrine of Signatures says that God visually patterned nature in such a way as to provide insight into how a plant should be used. For example, if a root was knotted, it was considered likely that this particular root could be applied in magic to bind the spirit of sickness. Likewise, if a particular leaf was porous, perhaps it was intended by the Divine to heal problems with pores in the skin.

Beyond the visual appearance of a plant, the Doctrine of Signatures also talks about the significance of color and texture. Flowers, roots, or other plant parts that produce a red juice could often be used in aiding blood-related conditions, while those that had a yellow hue could be applied to cases of jaundice. Seeds that were particularly hard might be used in curatives for kidney stones, and a leaf with a rough surface might be applied to a similarly rough skin condition.

In this last example, we see the Law of Similars (of like affecting like) taken very literally. The Doctrine of Signatures is tied pretty closely to this concept. While some healers might consider opposites, like cool-colored plants to aid fever, most looked for likenesses. The relationship between these two metaphysical theories has remained strong over the years, and you will see many examples of both Signatures and Similars throughout this material.

For the most part, the Doctrine of Signatures was used in the herbal arena for healing. However, there are historical examples that were a little more creative and better suited to use as a prototype for modern Green Witchery. In one account, heart-shaped petals or leaves were used to strengthen a broken heart and for love magic. Another written record says that maidenhair was used to make a person's hair more luxurious.

It seems that today's Green Witch has a lot more options available than we previously thought. If a spell calls for a flower or plant to which you have no access, the Doctrine of Signatures and Law of Similars says you can substitute an item of a similar shape, texture, or color and still maintain magical congruency. For example, peace charms often include lavender as a component. If you have no lavender, you could substitute another pale blue flower or a very smooth leaf. The blue hue emphasizes harmony and the smooth texture paves the way for smooth relationships.

With all this in mind, let's look at Magical Sympathy next. This principle states that things act on one another over a distance because they're linked together in life's network. This action or effect can work through imitation, such as using a lemon or a mandrake root as a poppet to represent the person or animal to whom the magic is directed. Imitation relates strongly to Signatures and Similars because we're looking at appearances and likenesses again for insights about applying that plant magically.

Sympathy can also work through what's called *contagion*. An ancient example of contagion would be rubbing curative aloe gel on the blade of a weapon that had caused a wound, with the intention of indirectly curing that wound. Since this particular example is kind of outdated, we can adapt the concept to today's reality fairly easily.

Let's say you know you hurt someone by your words. To magically open communication again and begin the healing process, you might rub your lips with a homemade rosewater balm. White roses in particular emphasize peace, and applying this to your lips puts the healing energy on the source of the problem. As you can see, Magical Sympathy provides creative Green Witches with still more options and choices to mix and mingle our magic to perfection.

Practical Considerations

When all is said and done, Green Witches are a very pragmatic lot. If one plant or flower is not available, they find another item to substitute or look to dried plants instead. Don't be afraid to follow this tradition in your magical undertakings, bearing in mind that Sympathy and Signatures can give you some good ideas of where to begin.

NOTE: When I first started practicing Green Witchery, I discovered that there are some practical considerations in this art. For example, how much room do you have available for gardening and storage? Green magic has this way of taking over entire rooms and significant parts of yards if you don't plan ahead (and sometimes even when you do).

Generally, I suggest starting small with a window box garden and a shelf on which to store your harvested plants (you can always expand later once you're more proficient with green magic). You'll also need some dark jars with good sealing lids (like kitchen canisters) and labels. Believe me when I say that one dried plant looks a lot like another, so label all your jars inside and out. Be sure to include any special information about the plant (like its harvesting time or unique magical attributes that develop from growing conditions). As your collection grows, it's helpful to store the plants in alphabetical order so you can find them quickly.

CORE PLANTS

The Green Witch's plant collection seems to begin with some standards. I can't imagine a Green Witch without rose petals, for example. Roses are truly the queens of the flower kingdom, and have so many magical applications that it's difficult to list them all! Also, flowers like lavender, clover, daisy, and woodruff all rank high, because they're easy to locate and used in literally hundreds of spells each. Similarly, in the herb category, rosemary, sage, garlic, mint, and vanilla are all common and easily stored for up to a year in a dark, cool area without losing magical potency. For trees, I suggest hawthorn, pine, birch, and willow for serviceability. Among fruits and vegetables, oranges, lemons, beans, berries, and beets are good starting points.

I don't expect you to run out to the supermarket or cooperative and get all this right away. Nor do I expect you to run outside and dig up whatever yard space you may have. Take your time and build your Green Witch kit as time, space, and money allows. Do it slowly and thoughtfully, gathering or growing only those things that you feel you'll use regularly, and that have applications in the greatest number of magical processes. This way, your art won't overwhelm your living space or your wallet.

By the way, Green Witches who have little or no space for growing their own plants and flowers are not doomed to mediocrity. You just have to be a little careful about where you get your components. Look for organic suppliers (cooperatives are often very good for this, as are health food stores) of plants, flowers, and fruit. Make sure your suppliers are knowledgeable and responsible with their products. In other words, make sure they know what they're selling and have proper precautions noted for things that could harm pets, those who are pregnant, and so forth. Also, look around in the store: Are the fresh flowers, plants, and/or herbs bright and perky looking? Is the place clean and free of insects? If so, you've probably found a good outlet.

Now, just because you haven't sown or harvested your plants at special times to improve their energies, it doesn't mean you can't still use the timing ideas I provided earlier. Instead, wait until an auspicious moment to weave your magic or mingle ingredients. Consider preserving (drying, putting in dark glass bottles, freezing, or whatever) at similarly positive times. Or, charge your flowers and plants in sunlight or moonlight for a symbolic number of hours. This way, you can still bring an extra supportive dimension to your green magic without completely rearranging your living space.

TOOLS OF THE TRADE

Along with favored flowers and plants, the Green Witch usually has a collection of tools they prefer. These aren't magical tools like an athame or chalice, per se, but they do take on a special air when being wielded by the Green Witch in their work. Since I've tinkered as a Green Witch for about fourteen years now, I have a pretty good idea of the kinds of implements you'll want to gather for yourself for starters. These are:

MEASURING TOOLS: Some types of green magic, specifically the spells that go from garden to table, require some precision. A standard set of measuring spoons and cups is fine.

A SHARP KNIFE: You may want to have a couple of these: one used for edible items and one for inedible flowers and plants, so the two never accidentally mix. You can also consider a ritual knife for this purpose, leaving it on your altar between uses to gather supportive energy.

A WOODEN SPOON: I've always felt that a Green Witch without a wooden spoon is almost as naked as one without jewelry! This particular tool comes from nature's storehouse, too, and mixing magical ingredients with a wooden spoon instead of plastic is preferable (plastic is magically "dead"). Because wood is porous, you may want to have several of these, as I suggested with knives, keeping each one separated by the types of plants and flowers (or preparations) you use to blend and serve the magic.

MIXING CONTAINERS: While wooden bowls are nice, in this case, I suggest using stoneware bowls. They are very easy to clean and they're effectively nonporous. If you can only afford one, that will be enough. Remember that a mixing bowl is a good representation of the Goddess, too, as it represents a womb, and it is a viable substitute for a chalice on the altar.

POTS AND PANS: Most Green Witches prefer to have a separate set of pots and pans to make their preparations. I do not recommend aluminum for your purposes as it seems to adversely affect the process. Properly seasoned cast-iron pans, and any other type of cookware, are better choices. Again, in the interest of safety, you may want to keep the pans used for nonedible preparations separate.

STORAGE CONTAINERS: Glass over plastic wherever serviceable. Dark glass is much better for almost all plants and flower parts because it protects them from sunlight (this eliminates the aroma and dries out the essential oils). Whatever containers you choose, find ones that can easily be labeled and that have air-tight lids. The air-tight lids will also increase your preserved greenery's shelf life.

JUNK BOX: Not a necessity, but a handy thing to have for all kinds of magic. Keep a basket, box, drawer, baggie, or food storage container filled with things like rubber bands, ribbon, glue, glitter, fabric scraps, paper clips, tweezers, spare scissors, thread, yarn, needles, pins, and stickers. You'll gain a better understanding of how these kinds of things are useful in the remainder of this material.

MISCELLANY: There are some other things I've found particularly useful to the Green Witch's toolkit. First is cheesecloth, which can protect plants from certain insects. This can also be used with straining or drying techniques. You can buy cheesecloth at a well-stocked supermarket. Fillable tea bags or drawstring cotton bags that can be used as sachets, bath balls, and the like are also ideal to have on hand. Next, we come to sifters, strainers, drying screens, and a blender or food processor. Sifters will help you achieve congruity in your incenses and powders; strainers are very helpful in teas, tinctures, potions, and brews; drying screens are for those of you who are going to grow or buy fresh plants and then preserve them at home; and a good blender or food processor is another way of achieving even-sized plant pieces and/or mixing things to perfection.

GARDENING TOOLS: For those readers planning to grow their own flowers and plants, you'll probably want to gather a small shovel, weed puller, gardening scissors (this can become an alternative athame in your sacred space), trowel and fork to break up and aerate the soil, and gloves (optional). Also consider getting some type of landscaping fabric to combat weed infestation. We'll talk about this more specifically when we explore the subject of magical gardens.

As with your flower and plant kit, I don't really expect you'll gather everything on this list at once. Some things you should already have around the house; others, you can find inexpensively (as the budget allows) at dollar stores, second-hand shops, and the supermarket. And by all means, don't forget the internet. Suppliers of organic herbs and flowers often have the implements you need, too.

Giving Back to the Earth

A final, but vital, aspect of Green Witchery is remembering to give something back to the Earth that has so generously provided for and sustained our magic. Exactly what constitutes this "something" is up to you. Here are some possibilities:

- Create and execute monthly spells and rituals that focus energy toward re-greening the Earth.
- Place a crystal or other natural token at the base of a plant when you harvest its petals, leaves, or roots.
- Prepare organic, magically enhanced fertilizers for the soil where you live (even if you're not gardening, this is a great gift for the planet). One good approach is to compost (this neatly recycles, too). When you have enough organic matter, charge the mixture with an incantation before adding it to the soil. The only caution here is to check local ordinances about the type of container you will need for composting legally.
- Sow a seed to replace any plants that you harvest fully (root and all). Note that you can do this even if you're buying the entire plant somewhere—just go to a field and scatter seeds to the winds, or plant some in the ground at a local park.
- Say a prayer for the plant or commune with its spirit before you harvest any part of it. This is one way of respectfully requesting permission from the nature spirits to harvest what you need.
- Recycle anything you can, so that extra flowers and plants need not be wasted. For example, if you've used flower oils in your candles, save the wax remnants, melt them together, and re-create new candles. The wax should have retained some of the original aroma, so less flower oil will be needed in a new batch. Another good hint for Kitchen Witches is to freeze vegetable ends and pieces to make soup stock rather than

harvesting fresh vegetables. Then, when you're done with these, recycle them even further by using them as a great base for your magical garden's compost.

If every spiritually-minded person in the world were to follow through on two to three of these suggestions regularly, our Earth would begin healing far more quickly. The thoughtfulness and regard toward the Earth that these actions represent are good role models for others, especially our children. From here, the tradition of tending and keeping the Earth grows outward, taking root in future generations.

CHAPTER 3

Magical Gardens

"To cultivate a garden is to walk with God."
—CHRISTIAN N. BOVEE

Earlier, I talked about how a plant's growing conditions can dramatically affect its magical properties. What better way to know for sure under what circumstances your magical flower and plant components were grown and harvested than to do it yourself? This material is dedicated to growing and harvesting, be they indoor plants, windowsill pots, a small yard garden, a fancy fairy-attracting plot, or a full formal array.

For those of you who bear the proverbial black thumb, have no fear. I used to have the same problem. What I've discovered is that being a Green Witch helps you develop a similarly green thumb. Also, we need to remember that what we perceive as "killing" a plant is really because of our lack of knowledge about how to care for that plant, or external circumstances over which we have little control (like curious cats). Both of these problems have resolutions!

If you find your plants are not thriving, ask a local florist to refer you to a good book on plants that includes gardening information (my book, *The Herbal Arts*, is one example;

another good option is *The Garden Encyclopedia*, published by Wm. H. Wise & Co.). Check the type of soil the plant requires, how much sunlight it needs, and how much water it should receive. The two most common mistakes are drowning the plant, or just the opposite: not watering it enough.

A third common error is putting shade plants in a sunny location. While some "sun" plants will do fairly well in partial shade, the opposite is not true for shade plants—sunlight damages their greenery and will eventually kill them. So, if you get any literature with your plants (like those little growing guide spikes), *read it!* You may find your thumb changes color pretty quickly.

As for difficulties with children and pets, I've solved mine by putting indoor plants in locations well out of reach of little hands and paws (except the catnip, of course). Outside, I've added small white fences that were very inexpensive and just enough of a deterrent to keep the dog from jumping in and digging (not to mention keeping the kids from harvesting the vegetables before they ripen!).

If you follow these simple guidelines, you'll find success as a gardener. I would also recommend that new gardeners start out simply; don't try to do too much too soon. Learn how to properly cultivate one or two specific plants before taking on a larger garden. For example, if you love roses and want to use them for magic, cultivate one or two rose species (there are lots to choose from). When they have established themselves and are thriving, try a different plant or flower. The knowledge you gained during your first effort naturally makes the second one more successful.

There's another advantage to this approach: because you've worked closely with one particular type of flower or plant, you're going to be more naturally attuned to its energies. It will be easier to commune with that plant's spirit, and you'll feel more confident about the ways in which you apply it to other areas in your magical arts.

Practical Considerations

Before I start talking about various types of gardens, I want you to seriously think about how much time and space you have available. Gardening, big and small, is an ongoing effort. You cannot expect to have a lush garden if you regularly forget to water and weed because of business deals, playful children, or other obligations. Similarly, you can't neglect plants magically if you want them to have the right energy for the purposes you have planned. I'm not saying this to discourage you, but because I'm busy, too! I spend many hours of my week just keeping up landscaping, one indoor garden, and several outdoor gardens. We all have obligations and duties. Gardening is a joy for me, but for another person, it could be a nightmare. There's nothing more aggravating and discouraging than planting a beautiful bit of greenery, and then finding you have no time to enjoy it. The garden becomes overgrown, weedy, or sickly. Know yourself well enough and be honest with yourself about whether you have the tenacity and the time that gardening requires.

If you decide to forge ahead, the next consideration is the type of soil you have to work with (indoor gardeners don't have to worry about this one). I live in an area with lots of clay, for example, and only certain plants take well to that base. So, if you wanted to sow something not suited to clay soil, you'd have to look into getting replacement topsoil for your garden. If you're not sure what kind of soil you have, ask your local garden shop or a local college's cooperative extension service. You may also be able to find this information online, but always ensure that you're doing research through reliable sources.

Next, look at your available light. Indoor gardeners, what parts of your home get direct and indirect sunlight? What type of flower box or planter do you plan to create (and how much space is available for them)? Outdoor gardeners, look at your yard. What part of it gets the most sun? What part gets the least? Where do you want the garden to go, and how big will you make it? You might want to even sketch the layout for your yard, drawing plants and rocks where you think you'd like them to go. Once you answer these questions, you can choose plants suited to the size, light, climate zone, and soil of the garden you're creating.

I know all this sounds very mundane, and you're most likely anxious to get into the magic of it, but one really does affect the other. If you haven't paid attention to the practical considerations of gardening, no amount of magic will make your flowers and plants flourish. Green Witches make every effort to work within natural laws, following the Mother's lead. Nature shows us where to sow things…just go look at a forest! Some plants tuck their roots neatly beneath lush, larger plants so they get shade. Others stand brazenly out in the sun. This is Mother Earth's gardening blueprint, and if we follow that pattern conscientiously, we'll rarely go wrong.

Tooling Around

Earlier, I mentioned various tools that are useful to Green Witches. This section continues to look into other materials you may need. I've included things that you might not immediately think of as implements, like fertilizers and fences. But, these items are very useful in the Green Witch's gardening kit too.

Please also realize that since a Green Witch works with the Earth, these tools are just as sacred to them as implements of the altar (if you choose to think of them that way). For example, the border of your garden equals the boundary of the sacred space. The fertilizer is like positive energy to your plants, markers can equate to elemental correspondences, and so forth. Be creative!

With this in mind, remember to cleanse your tools by moving the item through a purifying incense like sage or cedar, sprinkling them with spring water or lemon water, or other similar techniques. Charge them in sunlight (this energy is directly connected to plant growth), and say a prayer over them so that your personal God or Goddess will bless your efforts.

Decorative Items

This generally applies to outdoor gardens, but creative indoor gardeners can use them, too. Nurseries carry a wide variety of decorative landscaping and gardening items, some of which are perfectly suited to magic (like images of gods and goddesses or fairy folk). Decorative items highlight the theme of your garden, accent visual beauty, can be used to direct earth energies, and evoke smiles from onlookers.

For example, I have the following decorations around my yard: a fountain with crystals, two stoneware dragons, a hummingbird bell (near the berry plants), a birdhouse with bath and feeder nearby, a pagoda, a Chinese stone lantern, a replica of the Buddha, small standing stones (taken out of the yard during drainage), hanging flower pots, two large lions that guard our door, and a stoneware bunny (we have a lot of baby bunnies around here). I didn't get all of these at once. It's been an ongoing process of looking for just the right items to put in specific places.

Obviously, a decorative item isn't a "tool." However, it is one that landscapers will find particularly useful in illustrating magical ideals or themes without a word!

Fencing or Borders

Fences and borders can be used to keep unwanted visitors out of your gardens or simply as decoration. Some options are fist-sized, water-worn stones that make a very nice permanent border; logs or thick branches cut from a fallen tree also make a nice border, but will biodegrade after a while; wooden and plastic fences; and stackable brick pieces or molded concrete blocks are readily available at garden and hardware stores for very reasonable prices.

Finally, there are some plants called "border plants" that can be used to create a natural border around your garden. These are worth considering if you're not worried about animals or children getting into things. Examples of border plants include evergreens (large and small), deciduous shrubs, begonias, garden mums, dwarf feverfew, and sweet alyssum. In an herb garden, dill, anise, basil, and savory are good options.

FERTILIZERS

By definition, a fertilizer is a substance added to hasten growth, augment plant yield or size, and improve overall soil condition. Note that a fertilizer is not a synonym for plant food, since plant food only nourishes the flora and does not improve the soil.

Thankfully, there are a lot of natural fertilizers from which to choose, not the least of which is your own compost or a homemade mixture. Some items that could be blended for fertilizer include fish oil (like what you drain off tuna); vegetable ends and pieces, cut small; ground up bones (you can use a food grinder); eggshells; ash from a fireplace; and coffee grounds (these also deter ants). Other options are shrub cuttings, lawn clippings, fallen leaves, and sawdust from carpentry efforts.

For those who would prefer to buy a ready-made fertilizer, there are many available. The key to choosing fertilizers for your garden really comes down to reading labels. See what kinds of flowers and plants will benefit from a particular fertilizer, and if you're not sure, ask!

HAND TOOLS

Hand tools probably bear the closest similarities to what we normally think of as magical implements. The trowel might be considered a kind of wand, your gardening scissors an athame, and so forth. Small rakes, hoes, and weed pullers are also good implements to have readily available.

If you're planting a very large garden, you may want to consider getting a rototiller for turning and preparing your soil. You'll still need hand tools, but this will make the initial process go a little faster.

Insect Repellents

The Green Witch knows that insects can be a tremendous boon to a garden by collecting and sharing various types of pollen and spores. Insects can also be a horrendous bane, eating up roots, leaves, flowers, vegetables, and so on, or blighting them with eggs. Because the Green Witch honors the Earth, this is not a rules-be-damned mission. Insecticides are not an option with plants you want to use for magic, nor if you wish to maintain an Earth-first outlook. So, what do you do?

One option is to learn companion planting techniques. Companion plants help each other grow and help deter pests. The following is a list of examples of what to grow when plagued with pests:

- ANTS: Plant mint near cabbages and tomatoes
- APHIDS: Plant chives around your carrots and roses, marigolds near the tomatoes or potatoes, and mustard near bean plants.
- JAPANESE BEETLES: Plant tansy near the berry bushes.
- SNAILS: Plant rosemary near the beans.
- WHITEFLY: Plant thyme near eggplant, potatoes, and tomatoes.

Beyond companion planting, there is always the option of making homemade insect repellents. Perhaps the simplest is a tomato leaf tincture: steep tomato leaves in warm water and repeat until heady with aroma. Most insects don't like tomatoes, and grabbing a few leaves off these plants won't hurt them. To boost the effect of the tincture, add other aromatic plant parts like chamomile and rosemary leaves, onion slices, and marigold petals. Apply after every rainstorm, using a spray applicator.

By the way, this Earth-first approach goes for other pests too. For example, I just ignore the rear strawberry patch. The bunnies have "claimed" this area, but leave everything else alone, so I don't complain. I could, however, put hair clippings, garlic, marigold, and onions in that area (rabbits don't like those aromas).

Finally, one thing I've found particularly helpful for deterring most insects (other than wood ants) is wood shavings. Specifically, I mix cedar and hemlock together and put a good amount around the base of all my plants. Come fall, this makes great mulch to turn back into the soil, thereby enriching it over the winter.

Markers

These are most helpful for those of you who want to create kitchen gardens so you know where various herbs or vegetables have been placed. Even when things start growing, it's often hard to tell sprouts apart, so I usually push a stick through the seed package and put it in the soil at the back of a row. Some garden shops sell stoneware signs for herbs and flowers that are quite pretty, but rather expensive unless you plan on sowing that particular plant every year. Instead, for the budget-minded garden Witch, another alternative is writing the name of the flora on old popsicle sticks in waterproof marker. These will last for at least a season.

Support Trellises or Spikes

These are necessary for vining flowers like clematis, vegetables like cucumbers, peas, and beans, and heavy-topped plants like tomatoes. Clematis, in particular, is a lovely addition to outdoor gardens because you can put it in as a backdrop, then pattern the ground around it in the front. Try fashioning your own trellis like a magical rune or other symbolic shape so that the energy represented by that pattern grows with your vining plants!

Weed Deterrents

While there are such things as helpful or useful weeds, most gardeners consider them a pain. From a magical perspective, pull weeds working through your garden's surface counter-clockwise (for banishing). If you can do this during the waning or dark moon, all the better.

But, do you really want to spend time pulling out creeping plants, dandelions, and other unwanted guests in our gardens when you could be enjoying them instead? My solution to this problem has been to use landscaping fabric wherever possible. I put small, anchored strips between rows of seeds or seedlings (this also neatly marks the rows). Large pieces are laid over any dirt readied for a decorative garden, with holes cut where I want the flora to go.

To finish everything off, we also need to consider what I call "fillers." Most folks who use landscaping cloth wouldn't want it to be visible. So, I just sprinkle landscaping rock or mulch over the surface of the fabric to cover it. Nurseries often carry a variety of stones and bark (call ahead and ask to be sure) that can also be used as filler. Choose a color or size that's visually appealing or magically significant. Like-wise, department stores, hardware stores, home and garden suppliers, and so on often have summer garden shops with a variety of mulches (cocoa shells are particularly pretty and have an amazing aroma). Do, however, shop around. Prices at these places vary dramatically, and price doesn't always ensure quality.

Magical Augmentations

After all the rather mundane considerations of gathering tools together, you're probably more than anxious to get your hands dirty with a little magic. What I've assembled here are some of the methods I've used successfully over the years, and those that I feel are fairly adaptable no matter the size of your garden.

- Magical land blessings were customary in a variety of cultures, taking place just prior to sowing or sometimes following the harvest. In Rome, they sprinkled holy water on the ground while walking the entire tract of land, or danced the fields in white robes. In China, offerings of grain, wine, and fruits were left for the spirits of the land. In Germany, people gathered a small amount of dirt from the four-quarters of the garden and mixed it with oil, milk, and honey, saying "Be fruitful, multiply, and fill the Earth" (a Christianized incantation). Following these examples, find some personally significant way to magically ready your land for the work ahead before you start.

- Sow clockwise from the center of your garden outward. Do this, too, whenever you're preparing the soil. Native American tradition says this nurtures plant spirits.

- For indoor plants and window arrays, hang a crystal whose energies correspond to the flower or plant over the pot so the flora can grow toward it and be augmented by that vibration. For example, lavender seems enriched by amethyst.

- Put blessed crystals in the soil at the four corners of a garden or planter to create a sacred space for your flora. Alternatively, use charged crystals in the base of a planter for drainage and to create a magical foundation from which your flora will grow. If you're not familiar with the difference between blessing and charging, hang tight: you can find such information in future material.

- If you're going to graft a bud or shoot, lunar gardening instructs us to cut the graft during Capricorn and attach it during Pisces.

- Moss agate is considered the Green Witch's best ally for fertile fields. Wear it when you tend your garden or add to the soil. Lodestone and copper are also said to improve your yield if put around the perimeter of the garden (for potted plants and window boxes, you can wrap copper wire around the pot's edge to create an energy circuit).

- If you're growing magical herbs, tradition tells us that they will be most powerful if harvested on Midsummer's Day. Do not use an iron cutting tool, however. This will cut away the herb's magical properties. A wheat cake is a suitable offering to thank the herb spirits for their gift.

- Throughout the gardening season, be cautious about working weather magic. If possible, work with the weather that Mother Earth gives you. Should a drought or flood condition occur, you can consider attracting rain or sun to your area briefly as a relief method. Tossing kelp in the air, shaking a rain stick in the air, sprinkling water, and scattering rice are three methods of attracting rain. Of course, carrying an umbrella is almost a sure-fire folk method for encouraging a day of sunshine (umbrellas, when opened, represent the solar disk).

   However, bear in mind that any such spells or rituals can disrupt weather patterns far beyond your scope of awareness. This may not be really suited to the Green Witch's domain.

- When you're ready to harvest the first thing from your garden (first fruits), have a special ritual and give a part back to the land. The Hopi tell us that this act of thankfulness assures ongoing abundance.

- Sing and chant while you tend your soil. This fills the air with good vibrations (and plant spirits enjoy music). If you're feeling particularly creative, try to match the theme of your vocalization to the magic you're growing.

- Fertilize your magical energy regularly. Place your hands palms down over the garden or planter and visualize it being filled with a bright light whose color suits your magical goal (like pink for friendship or red for love).

- Learn a little about what planets rule your flora, as it might help your gardening efforts. For example, if you notice that Mars is very prominent in the night sky, it might be a good time to plant or harvest tarragon, garlic, onion, pepper, radish, or basil (all of which are governed by Mars) to improve their energies. Here are a few other correspondences (more may be found in the Correspondence List in this book's Appendix):

SUN: Saffron, chamomile, sunflower, rosemary, marigold

MOON: Melons, water lilies, willow, lettuce

MERCURY: Carrot, marjoram, caraway, fennel

VENUS: Tomato, periwinkle, violet, strawberry

JUPITER: Clove, anise, nutmeg, sage, dandelion

SATURN: Elm, pine, barley

- When growing apple trees, it's customary to give them a libation of apple mead or juice at harvest time. This pleases the spirit of the tree and encourages ongoing abundance for you (and the crop).
- Nettle and dock are considered magically paired, as are beans and squash, and parsley and mint. Growing these together improves the energies of both.

NOTE: Do not sow mint unless you want a lot of it. Or sow it in a pot or planter box to limit its spread.

- Having a small bit of bramble, or any thorny bush, around your garden acts as a protective field, snagging unwanted energies before they reach your plants.

- Walking the land with burning sage or cedar will clear it of any unwanted vibrations and temporarily chase away insects.
- If you find any large stones when cultivating the soil, set these aside. You can use them to make small dolmens or stone circles, place them at the corner points of the garden as guardians, or put them around the yard to watch over the land.
- When you have a question laying heavy on your heart, go to your garden and close your eyes. Randomly take hold of a leaf or flower. Then, open your eyes to see what type of plant it comes from and use the magical correspondences as interpretive values. Let's say you're wondering about how good a relationship was, and you plucked a daisy, I'd say things were iffy (you're questioning whether or not love is true).

As you can see, the magical potential for improving the energies in your garden, and adding them to your other magical methods, is fairly diverse. You have a lot of room to add personal touches, which makes it all the more fulfilling.

Gardening by the Moon

Even as recently as one hundred years ago, you could still find farmers watching the moon's phases and signs to be sure their gardens would thrive. A Green Witch often falls back on this information to improve the overall fertility of their fields, and the basic energies of each plant sown. Here's a brief review of some guidelines to get you started:

MOON IN ARIES: Plant only garlic and onions.

MOON IN TAURUS: Plant potatoes or leafy vegetables.

Moon in Gemini: Weed and cultivate. Do not plant or transplant.

Moon in Cancer: Graft, transplant, sow, or force budding. This is a very productive sign.

Moon in Leo: Focus on ridding your garden of unwanted insects or weeds.

Moon in Virgo: Fairly barren. Don't do any extensive gardening during this sign other than basic maintenance.

Moon in Libra: Sow flowers, root crops, vines, and lettuce.

Moon in Scorpio: Excellent for promoting plant growth, so fertilize now.

Moon in Sagittarius: Productive for onions.

Moon in Capricorn: Plant tubers and root crops only.

Moon in Aquarius: Cultivate and turn the soil.

Moon in Pisces: Excellent for flora requiring good root growth.

First Quarter: Plant leafy annuals with above-ground yields like broccoli, cauliflower, celery, spinach, and lettuce.

Second Quarter: Plant rounded flowers and plants like cantaloupe, eggplant, peas, tomatoes, and cucumbers.

Third Quarter: Sow bulbs, root crops, beets, garlic, carrots, and anything else that has an underground yield. Also, fruit bushes seem to do well when planted during this phase.

FOURTH QUARTER: Turn the soil, weed, and eliminate pests. This is most effective when combined with the moon signs of Leo, Virgo, or Gemini. If you're harvesting during this moon phase, try to time it for the signs of Aquarius, Aries, Gemini, Leo, or Sagittarius.

It should be noted that every hour of the day, every day of the week, and each month also has magical significance that you could add to the lunar equation if you so desire. Here's a brief overview of the magical associations for weekdays and months for your reference:

WEEKDAYS

MONDAY: A fruitful day, especially for lunar-oriented plants.

TUESDAY: A high-energy day that will boost the energies in flowers or plants that improve physical vitality or mental keenness.

WEDNESDAY: A creative day, good for spiritually-centered flowers and plants.

THURSDAY: Another high-energy day, suited to flora that augments devotion or tenacity.

FRIDAY: An emotionally warm day, suited to plants that are used in love and fertility magic.

SATURDAY: Sow, harvest, or tend plants on this day that augment transformation, manifestation, and/or comprehension.

SUNDAY: The perfect day to work with solar-oriented flowers and plants.

Months

JANUARY: Bless the soil in which you'll be sowing protective plants.

FEBRUARY: Charge the soil in which you'll be growing health-related plants or those that motivate positive energy.

MARCH: Focus on plants and flowers associated with success and victory or those under the dominion of Mars.

APRIL: Work with lucky flowers and plants this month for a little serendipity.

MAY: All plants do well during this month as energy is directed toward progress and growth.

JUNE: Fridays in June double the loving, warm energies in relationship flowers and plants.

JULY: Combine your Sunday efforts with this month to geometrically increase the energy for leadership and self-awareness.

AUGUST: Work with plants and flowers that accentuate peace and harmony.

SEPTEMBER: A perfect month for working closely with your magical herbs and flowers.

OCTOBER: Consider transforming any of your flowers and plants into something else during this month (like oils, incense, potpourri). This is the month of useful changes!

NOVEMBER: Work with flora that's associated with psychic energies.

DECEMBER: Work with plants that have magical correspondences with wisdom, prudence, and spiritual awareness.

A Green Witch's Garden Patterns and Themes

A Green Witch's designs and choice of plants will depend much on what they hope to achieve and the available space. The options are broad, but here are a few ideas you can try. Just tailor them to suit your specific environmental conditions. Also, please don't let these examples limit your imagination. You can create many different gardens and garden patterns as long as you remember to customize the design to suit the flora you're using.

Since I don't know how much space each of you has for your gardening efforts, the ideas can be adapted to almost any situation. Just increase or decrease the number/type of plants you use. The most important thing is to allow each bit of greenery the space, lighting, soil type, and water it needs to thrive. For example, some plants do not do well in low-lying zones because of dampness. So, if you wanted to use this kind of flower or plant in a wet region, you might want to design its planting area with an elevated mound to provide proper drainage. Keep this in mind as you set up your garden's layout.

Magical Gardens

As the name implies, a magical garden will be filled with either the flowers and plants you use most frequently for magic or those that are specifically associated with the magical arts. Thistles and wintergreen are good choices for clearing magic's path, rosemary and lily improve willful focus, and rowan (mountain ash) and carnation provide power. Additionally, marigold and thyme could be chosen for psychic ability, and gardenia sown for spiritual awareness.

In terms of patterning your magical garden, there is a plethora of magical styles, symbols, and patterns from which to choose. One obvious choice is a pentagram. Other options include laying the flowers out in the design of a favorite rune, hermetic emblem, Cabalistic lettering, or a symbol honoring your personal God or Goddess.

THE FAIRY GARDEN

This is one of my favorite gardens, because it inspires imagination and whimsy, and also invokes the muse. Fairy gardens work well on a small scale (after all, these beings are sometimes called "wee folk" even though their power is not small, by any means). For a general array of plants, those said to please the Fey include clover, heather, hawthorn, hazel, oak, ash, primrose, roses, straw (use this as mulch), strawberries, and thyme. Whatever you plant should be set into a circle, making a beautiful fairy ring!

If you want to attract a particular type of fairy to your garden, you'll need to consider the element with which that fairy is associated and what plants come under that elemental domain. Here are some ideas:

WATER FAIRIES: (undines, Nakki, Vestri, etc.) Make sure to have a bird bath, fountain, or other water source in this garden. Flower and plant choices include: grapes, catnip, chamomile, spearmint, thyme, aster, birch, crocus, daffodil, daisy, foxglove, gardenia, heather, iris, lily, morning glory, mosses, pansy, and willow.

EARTH FAIRIES: (gnomes, elves, dwarves, etc.) Rocks and rich soil help to make up this garden. Flora choices include: alfalfa, mushroom, peas, sorrel, vervain, ferns, honeysuckle, ivy, magnolia, oleander, primrose, and tulips.

AIR FAIRIES: (sylphs, cloud people, Austri, etc.) Include a gathering of feathers or wind chimes in this garden. Choices for plants include: beans, mulberry, parsley, lemongrass, marjoram, mint, sage, savory, clover, dandelion, lavender, meadowsweet, pansy, and violet.

FIRE FAIRIES: (salamanders, hobs, Penates, etc.) Try to include some kind of solar imagery in this garden, perhaps a pot that features a sun in splendor. Choices for greenery include: chives, squash, sloe, basil, dill, garlic, lavage, rosemary, cactus, carnation, hawthorn, juniper, marigold, poppy, snapdragon, sunflowers, and thistle.

Once you've set up your fairy garden, it's a good idea to leave out small token offerings to encourage either visitors or permanent residents. Honey cakes and ale or sweet cream are traditional for this purpose.

THE MEDITATION GARDEN

My first thoughts on the design of this garden were that of the mandala, which represents the self, the spirit, and the great human capacity to live beyond our perceived boundaries. For those who are unsure about how to create such a pattern, please refer to my book *Labyrinth Walking* (Citadel/Kensington, 2001) for more insights.

The meditation garden might be created in two distinct ways. The first is simply to use plants and flowers that visually, spiritually, or aromatically motivate or deepen your meditative state. Examples of flora known for this effect are hyacinth, magnolia, lavender, and gardenia. Feel free to use any others that are personal favorites.

The second approach is a Zen rock garden. This garden is predominantly made of sand and various-sized stones with only occasional plants mingled in as the energy flow dictates. One nice part about the Zen garden is the low level of maintenance. Remember when creating this type of garden that the sand can also be "designed" using rakes and other tools so that it bears a rippled texture or specific magical pattern.

DYE GARDEN

If you're interested in making homemade dyes for your magical wardrobe, grow things like dock (black), marigold (yellow and orange), broom (green), wode (indigo/blue), saffron (yellow), madder (yellow-green), zinnia (greenish-gray), and safflower (red).

Aromatherapy Garden

There are two ways to think of this garden theme. The first is that of a personal sacred space, where the energy of the aromatics lifts your spirits. In this case, you'll want to plant this garden with flowers and herbs geared to your specific needs. Here's a brief aromatherapy correspondence list:

Basil: love, peace

Bayberry: prosperity

Gardenia: harmony, healing, love

Hyacinth: tranquility

Lavender: sex appeal (traditionally used to attract a male partner), restfulness

Lilac: unity, accord; psychism

Magnolia: meditative focus

Narcissus: vitality, self-image

Rose: love (all kinds, including self-love)

Rose Geranium: courage, banishing negativity

Rosemary: spell turning, mental clarity

Sweetpea: friendship, amiability, joy

Vervain: abundance, physical fertility

Violet: improved health, sex appeal (traditionally used to attract a female partner)

The second approach to this theme garden is to plant those flowers and herbs that you use regularly in making your magical oils, perfumes, incense, and potpourri. For this garden, the balm family, mint family, geraniums, roses, lavender, violets, and rosemary are all good options.

GODDESS IN THE GARDEN

For readers who follow a specific God or Goddess, this is a lovely, living reminder of your devotion and a great way to honor that being. For the center of your garden, get something that represents your God/dess (statuary comes immediately to mind). Around the being, sow the flowers and plants sacred to them. For example, someone who follows Hecate, the patroness of Witches, might put an image of her under a willow tree surrounded by dandelions, garlic, and lavender (all of which are under Hecate's dominion). Similarly, an image of Thor beneath the bows of a birch or oak tree surrounded by ox-eyed daisies and marjoram would be apt. The Correspondence List has more information on what plants are sacred to various gods and goddesses for your reference.

Hints and Helps

As you can probably tell, I do a lot of gardening. This wasn't always the case. There were many years in which I simply didn't have the time or space to really enjoy nature. Now that I can, I've kept track of some basic gardening tips that have proven helpful to me again and again. I think they'll help you, too:

- For annual gardens and vegetable gardens I highly recommend rotating your crops so that the soil doesn't lose specific nutrients. Different plants leach nutrients from the soil at different rates. Planting new types every few years gives the soil a chance to rebalance.

- If possible, let part of your garden fallow for one season (without planting anything in it). This gives the earth a breather and refreshes the soil.
- Buy your flowers, trees, shrubs, and so on from a reputable place that offers a one-year guarantee on some of their stock (this is particularly important for trees since these are expensive). Keep your receipts in a safe place.
- If you don't want to replace your flowers every spring, research perennial plants (these return every year). Annuals (these bloom for only one year) have a greater variety of sizes and colors (in my opinion) but they also require buying new plants each year. Perennials are a dollar-wise investment.
- To harvest flowers and plant parts for longevity and aromatic potency: barks are best collected early spring and late fall in long strips; roots should be taken with your autumn harvest; seeds need to be fully ripened, but picked before they fall off the plant; and herbs and flowers can be harvested almost any time, but early morning is best to ensure the aromatic appeal.
- If you have a limited amount of space at home, and want to dry your own herbs and flowers, there are several options available to you. The first is to purchase a three-foot length of netting and hang it from the ceiling in a dry, dark room. Place the plant parts on the net so they're not touching, and turn them regularly while drying. Similarly, you can string up a piece of clothesline, then bundle flowers and herbs together (blooms downward) off the line using clothespins. For the time-challenged Witch, another option is the microwave oven. Set it to approximately 20 percent power and put the herbs in for 20 seconds at a time. Turn them, and repeat until they achieve the desired texture. Be very careful; it's easy to burn them this way, but once you're done, you can just

store the dried plant parts in suitable containers. An oven set on low (200° F) is another safe option. Just make sure to check the plants regularly to prevent over-drying them.

All in all, I think (or hope) you'll find magical gardening to be a very fulfilling pastime. It is also one that puts the Green Witch back in touch with Mother Earth on an intimate basis. For those readers living in urban environments, this contact is very important and healthful—and for all those on a metaphysical path, staying in close communion with the Earth Mother's voice dramatically improves the results of your magic.

CHAPTER 4

Edible Petals and Blossoming Beverages

"What knowest thou of flowers except, belike,
to garnish meat with?"
—SHAKESPEARE, *HAMLET*

$\mathcal{M}$any flowers and plants in a Green Witch's garden are edible. Besides the sheer pleasure of eating things fresh from the garden, a Green Witch's motto is "think ahead." They will carefully consider how homegrown items can be applied in the magical pantry, and then sow the land accordingly.

At first, you might only think of vegetables, herbs, and fruits as items grown and harvested for the magical pantry, but many flowers are also edible and tasty. Historically, up until about 100 years ago, flowers were readily used in foods and beverages. This is a tradition the Green Witch can reclaim and one that represents a vitamin-rich source of magical symbolism besides!

To see where and how cooking with flowers began, we turn our attention to the East. China and Japan were probably among the first civilizations to discover the wonders of cooking and brewing with flowers. What better way to grace any lovely dish or sweet cup than the crowning glory of the natural world? I suspect Arabia and Egypt were likely participating in this tradition too, since the former held the profession of perfume-making in high regard, and the latter readily used flowers in religious rites, particularly embalming.

Later, during the Middle Ages, petal-laced beverages and foods made a huge impact on European culinary traditions. The interest in cooking and brewing with blossoms was most surely fueled by the magic-laden Asian flower lore and subsequently bolstered by the European love of gardening. Flower-garnished or flower-flavored salads, condiments, soups, meats, wines, and liquors (just to name a few) established a respectable place on the table alongside more traditional preparations. They were so admired, in fact, that flower cookery was a welcome addition to many royal gatherings. The custom of using flowers as a part of culinary endeavors went out of fashion over time, in part due to the advent of fast food, and in part due to the shift away from an agrarian society. Thankfully, herbalists have reawakened the public to many of the healthy benefits flowers provide. Roses, for example, have more vitamin C than oranges. This means that the Green Witch who chooses a vegetarian lifestyle will discover a wonderful source of dietary supplements in their garden—a source that also represents personal convictions!

I mention all this because I know some readers might be initially put off by the idea of eating or drinking flowers, as in some recipes given herein. I was, too, but now you can find me happily nibbling at roses or tossing some into a brew (which I can never keep in stock—it's constantly disappearing!). So give it a try.

NOTE: Make sure your flower source is organic and free of debris to ensure the best results.

Practical Considerations

In preparing your own flower and plant foods and beverages, two factors rise above all the others listed here as crucial for success. The first important factor is freshness. Flowers, fruits, herbs, and vegetables can be bought in preserved form when nothing else is available (practicality is part of the Green Witch's rulebook). But from a magical perspective, freshly harvested items bear a stronger energy signature that, in turn, increases your overall power.

To ensure freshness, gather your ingredients just prior to preparing them whenever possible. As you collect blossoms, make sure to get only the petals—no green parts—unless otherwise instructed by the recipe. These green parts can ruin the aroma or flavor of a dish. Also, remember to harvest your flowers just after the dew evaporates no later than 10:30 a.m. This way, the petals will have a higher concentration of essential oil (the oil is the most aromatic and savory part). Handle the petals carefully, storing them in a muslin or a nylon mesh bag, in a cool area, and use them as soon as possible. Once wilted, their taste is far less enjoyable. This also applies to leafy vegetables.

The second important consideration is temperature. Some types of flora are especially sensitive to heat. When starting a batch of brew with flower petals, for example, you do not boil as you would with many other preparations. Instead, I recommend gently simmering the petals until they turn translucent. This extracts the oils without burning. Slower cooking with vegetables yields more pleasant results as well, bringing out a full-bodied flavor that isn't often achieved in quickly prepared food.

A third consideration that people frequently overlook is physical sensitivity. Certain plants yield high amounts of pollen or other allergens. So, if you, or anyone for whom you're cooking are adversely affected by specific flowers or plants, I'd generally avoid those items. It's really not worth the risk. Find another edible flower or plant with similar magical correspondences that will work in the recipe instead.

Fourth, if you're not growing your own items, try to buy ones that are organic. Traces of chemical fertilizers or pesticides can taint or totally hinder magical methods. Also, make sure anything you cook with is free of everyday debris— any bits of mold, dirt, and the like. This is just common sense, but a quick rinse with cool water also has a spiritual cleansing quality that certainly wouldn't hurt!

Fifth, bear in mind time constraints and the theme of the magic. Choose your magical menus so they match your schedule, personal tastes, and needs. You will want to be able to focus on your goals rather than worrying over the hour, and edible magic won't do you much good if you don't *like* the food or beverage created!

Finally, as far as tools go, I believe you'll find just about everything you need to prepare these recipes right in your own kitchen. As with gardening, remember that magical cookery is a sacred art, so treat everything (measuring cups, a wooden spoon, the ingredients, and so forth) as you would the tools of your altar and you'll do just fine.

Magical Considerations

There's really nothing difficult about magical cooking and brewing. Since creating sacred space and generating magic ultimately begins with a different way of thinking and acting, the main adjustment you'll be making for pantry enchantments is your attitude while you cook or brew. We already talked about treating your kitchen tools a little differently, and that concept also goes for your working space. Approach it gently and thoughtfully, knowing this is a type of sanctuary. This is where you will whip up spiritual energy to perfection.

As you gather ingredients and blend them together, every step is now aimed at a specific theme. This is why I highly recommend that people do not try to make magical menus when they are angry or out-of-sorts. The negativity has a tendency to spill over into the food, which isn't what you want!

Besides shifting your demeanor to a semi-meditative, metaphysical mode, you'll also want to consider some of the methods used by our ancestors to improve the manifesting power of pantry enchantments. These methods include:

- Stirring a preparation clockwise to attract positive energy or counterclockwise to banish problems
- Preparing anything that rises or ferments during a waxing to full moon to ensure the successful preparation of the food or beverage
- Making an offering to one's hearth god or goddess before preparing any magical meals. This attracts that being's blessings, provides more positive energy with which to cook, and is even said to ensure the healthful qualities of your culinary efforts
- Leaving out gifts for the hob (the house fairy) who helps with brewing and cooking
- Sweeping the kitchen floor (using a broom) from the center outward to get rid of any lingering negativity
- Praying over the food or beverage as it's being prepared, or just prior to consumption
- Passing the food or beverage clockwise around the table for ongoing blessings to all those gathered there
- Having a candle burning while you cook or at the family table as a symbol of love and unity, or to honor the God/dess
- Burning incense that matches the goal of the magic you're whipping up in the food or beverage (this acts as an additional sensual cue that helps guide willpower)
- Playing music, singing, chanting, or dancing while you cook. No one ever said this couldn't be fun. In fact, joy is a powerful motivator for magic.

Obviously, these are but a few of the ways in which you can bring more magic into your kitchen. What's most important is that the actions and symbols you add to the "normal" cooking process have real meaning for you. When that happens, the magic flows just right. The results? Feeding body, mind, and soul from one platter or cup equally well!

Beverages

Most people who visit my home are greeted with some kind of beverage. Be it coffee, tea, soda, or homemade wines and beers, this seems to be the gesture of hospitality that I learned from my mother. Everyone has similar customs in their homes—little gestures that make people feel welcome. In this case, you're going to go one step further and make magically-enhanced beverages to suit the theme of any meeting or those that will spiritually help with fulfilling personal needs and goals.

I've tried to provide a sampling here of both alcoholic and nonalcoholic flower and plant beverages. Similarly, I've used ingredients that I felt might be readily found in the Green Witch's garden or on the pantry shelves. For more recipes along these lines, may I suggest my book: *A Witch Beverages and Brews* (1996) as one source?

PSYCHIC JUICE
FOR PROPHECY, INSIGHT, VITALITY, LOVE, AND SERVICE

HISTORY AND FOLKLORE: This beverage comes to us from Arabia where it is said that Mohammed gave birth to the main ingredient, rose geraniums, quite innocently by tossing his shirt over a mallow plant. In old folk traditions, a Green Witch would plant a specially enchanted rose geranium near their doorway to announce the arrival of guests. If you keep a pot of red geraniums in your home, it provides energy for health and safety, while the pink variety inspires love. The other flowers in this recipe have long been used in divination efforts.

- 1 quart apple juice (cider or sparkling cider are also options)
- 1 cup mixed marigold, pansy, and meadowsweet blossoms
- 1 cup sugar (or to taste)
- 1 lime, sliced
- 1 orange, sliced
- 8 rose geranium leaves

Warm the apple juice, sugar, and flower petals and leaves for five to ten minutes until sugar is dissolved. To this, add the sliced lime and orange and allow the mixture to cool. Strain and bottle the liquid, and place in the refrigerator until you wish to consume it. This can be served hot or cold (if hot, try adding an allspice berry or cinnamon stick). Keeps as long as typical apple juice.

ALTERNATIVE INGREDIENTS: Geraniums can be replaced with either dandelions or 6 whole bay leaves for similar magical results. Apple juice can be replaced with wine for a longer-lasting brew.

OTHER MAGICAL USES: Dab a bit of this drink on your doors or window sills to protect your home. Also, geraniums come in a variety of scents, so a mint geranium drink might be consumed for prosperity or passion, whereas a nutmeg geranium beverage could be quaffed for luck and devotion.

Yields 1 quart.

SERENDIPITY WINE
FOR GOOD FORTUNE AND IMPROVED HEALTH

HISTORY AND FOLKLORE: Honeysuckle, the main ingredient in this recipe, is also called woodbine in folk traditions. If honeysuckle suddenly starts growing near your home, it's a sign of improving luck. This plant spirit will also protect your family's health (the orange in this recipe accents the healthful qualities).

- 4 cups honeysuckle blossoms
- 1 gallon water
- 2 oranges, sliced and juiced
- ½ package wine yeast
- 6 cups sugar

Place the blossoms in a large crock. In another pot, warm one-half the gallon of water to just below boiling, then pour it over the petals. Allow this mixture to sit until the blossoms turn almost translucent. Strain and rewarm (to no more than 98° F) and the orange juice, sugar pieces, and yeast. Place into a fermentation container with a lock until the liquid becomes clear. A serviceable fermentation device can be made from an old glass wine bottle secured at the top with a balloon (be sure the bottle is clean). Strain off into smaller bottles and store in a cool, dark area for consumption. Keeps for a very long time.

ALTERNATIVE INGREDIENTS: Rose or violet petals are both considered very lucky and roses in particular augment vitality. You can decrease the number of flowers and steep them in grape juice with a bit of honey for a nonalcoholic alternative.

OTHER MAGICAL USES: Dab a bit on items that you carry for good fortune, or carry a small, well-sealed vial with you as a charm for luck. Pour out a libation of this wine during healing spells and rituals.

Yields 1 gallon.

FAIRY FOLK MEAD
FOR COMMUNING WITH DEVIC ENTITIES, FAIRY FOLK, AND PLANT SPIRITS

HISTORY AND FOLKLORE: Primroses were sometimes called fairy cups. Europeans believed that the wee people sometimes took shelter in this blossom during storms. Also called cowslips, this flower was among those considered sacred to Flora (Roman) and Chloris (Greek), both of whom make wonderful patronesses for Green Witches. The pinch of thyme in this recipe also invokes fairy energies.

- 2 quarts primrose heads
- 1 lemon
- 2 oranges
- 1 gallon water
- 3 pounds honey
- ½ package mead or wine yeast
- Pinch of thyme (optional)

Primroses can be brewed from dried petals quite effectively, or you can freeze fresh ones until you're ready to make this mead. Place the petals in a crock, and wash and peel the lemon and oranges, getting rid of as much pith on the rinds as possible. Place the rinds with the flowers, and squeeze the juices over the flowers and rinds.

In a separate pot, warm the water and honey together until the honey is dissolved. Bring to a boil for the next 10–15 minutes and skim any scum that rises to the surface. Cool for another 10–15 minutes before pouring this liquid over the flower mixture. Let cool to lukewarm, stirring regularly.

Next, add the yeast dissolved in one-quarter cup warm water and thyme. Cover with a towel and let the blend sit for five days, mixing it once a day. Strain and move the clear fluid to a glass container with a fermentation lock (or your makeshift one). When all signs of fermentation cease, decant and bottle.

ALTERNATIVE INGREDIENTS: Some folks like to add a touch of pineapple sage (about 2 tablespoons) to this mixture for a slightly zesty flavor.

Magically, this will provide you with the wisdom necessary for dealing effectively with plant spirits and devas. Two other ingredients you can consider adding are heather flowers and strawberries, both of which attract fairies and mingle well with the other ingredients.

OTHER MAGICAL USES: Leave a bit of this elixir in your fairy garden, or pour it out as a libation in any ritual, spell, or meditation that's focused on devic entities.

Yields 1 gallon.

ROMANTIC TEA
FOR UPLIFTING THE SPIRIT
OF LOVE AND BEAUTY

HISTORY AND FOLKLORE: The main ingredient in this tea, rose petals, has been used for thousands of years to motivate emotion. Ancient Greeks considered roses the primary symbol of love and beauty, having been born from the blood of Aphrodite. Cleopatra used roses to inspire Marc Anthony's adoration, and Romans often littered the floors of rooms with rose petals during marriage ceremonies. All the other ingredients in this recipe also have romantic or loving magical correspondences.

- 2 cups rose petals
- 2 cups water
- ½ teaspoon lemon balm
- ¼-in. ginger root, pounded
- Pinch rosemary (optional)
- Sugar or honey to taste
- 3 catnip leaves
- 1 orange slice
- Vanilla bean (for stirring)

Cover the rose petals with water and simmer over a low flame until the petals become translucent. Strain off the liquid, returning it to the original pan to warm with the remaining ingredients (except the vanilla bean and sweetener). Simmer until the liquid is heady with aroma, approximately 5 to 10 minutes. Pour into two cups and stir in sweetener using the vanilla bean. Enjoy with someone you love.

ALTERNATIVE INGREDIENTS: There are a lot of love flowers and spices that you can consider substituting, including: spearmint, thyme, raspberry (leaf, or fruit), marjoram, lemon or lime slices, lavender flowers, daisy petals, violets, and basil.

Other Magical Uses: If you make more of this, it's an excellent beverage to serve in a group setting to encourage unity and harmony. I also recommend it for handfasting rituals, magical engagement rites, and similar events.

Yields 2 cups.

SOLITARY MAY BOWL
For success, prosperity, and protection,
especially in battles

History and Folklore: The beautiful white woodruff blossoms are sacred to the Goddess, which is why it's featured in Beltane Wine (May 1). In pre-Christian times, woodruff scented a variety of drinks, and in the Middle Ages, it became popular as an overall tonic. Strawberries add a delightful flavor and magical joy to the equation.

- ½ handful of fresh sweet woodruff with blossoms
- 2–3 whole strawberries
- 3 cups cider or apple juice
- 1 orange slice
- 2 teaspoons sugar

Rinse the woodruff and fresh strawberries thoroughly. Place the rest of the ingredients together in a bowl and mix well. To increase the flavor, warm the cider or juice first. Chill the bowl for a minimum of one hour before straining and pouring into a large glass to enjoy. Garnish with berries. A great springtime refresher!

Alternative Ingredients: For a drink with greater spiritual cleansing qualities, add a slice of lemon in place of the orange and add one to two whole cloves. Both versions of this may be served hot with a stick of cinnamon.

OTHER MAGICAL USES: Carry a well-sealed vial of this with you as a charm that will attract victory and financial gain. If you wrap or dab some in leather, it will keep you from harm.

Yields 3 cups.

COMMUNICATION CORDIAL
FOR MESSAGE SPELLS, IMPROVED CONVERSATIONS, AND CONVINCING SPEECHES

HISTORY AND FOLKLORE: This beverage comes to us from Prussia in the Middle Ages, where it was made specifically to smooth speech and open the lines of communication. Cloves were favored then as a breath freshener and something to "sweeten" one's words.

- 1 cup of water
- 1 cup heather honey
- 1 small cinnamon stick
- 1 tablespoon vanilla extract
- 1 whole clove
- 2 cups vodka or rum

In a saucepan (preferably non-aluminum), bring the water to a low rolling boil. Add the remaining ingredients except for the alcohol, and stir regularly until the honey dissolves completely. Skim the froth off the surface and cool the liquid, then add the vodka and bottle it. I recommend letting the entire mix sit for 2 weeks before consuming.

ALTERNATIVE INGREDIENTS: To improve the power of speech, replace the vanilla with mint or almonds (the nuts can be put right into your storage bottle). You might also consider storing this beverage with a carnelian stone in the container (If you do, make sure to strain out the stone before drinking!). For a drink with greater spiritual cleansing qualities, add a slice of lemon in place of the orange and add one to two whole cloves. Both versions of this may be served hot with a stick of cinnamon.

OTHER MAGICAL USES: Dab a little of this on your lips or tongue before invoking the quarters or incanting a spell to communicate the message more effectively.

Yields 3 cups.

VEGETABLE AWARENESS
FOR PSYCHISM, ALERTNESS

HISTORY AND FOLKLORE: Most people have heard the old wives' tale that eating carrots will improve your eyesight. This recipe builds on that idea for the Green Witch wishing to improve their spiritual insights, adding radishes for energy and celery for concentration.

- 3 large carrots,
- 3 celery stalks
- 6 radishes
- 2 cups cabbage, diced

Dice the carrots and celery and slice up the radishes, then transfer them all to a blender, food processor, or juicer. Pulp the ingredients thoroughly. Strain the liquid through cheesecloth. The solids can go into your compost for the magical garden. This delicious beverage is a good source of beta-carotene, sodium, vitamin C, calcium, and potassium.

ALTERNATIVE INGREDIENTS: Try adding thyme or crushed bay leaves to this blend to increase the psychic flow of energy. You can also consider juicing some romaine lettuce, spinach, and dandelion flowers with this for growing oracular awareness.

OTHER MAGICAL USES: A fantastic drink to quaff over several days before attempting important divinatory efforts.

Yields 1-2 cups.

PEACEFUL-PETALED SODA POP
For harmony, symmetry, accord, acceptance

History and Folklore: All the flowers in this recipe were chosen because of their magical association with energies for compatibility, flexibility, and hospitality. Lavender generates tranquility, violets generate good-heartedness and heal old emotional wounds, and pennyroyal (a kind of mint) inspires peace between people or within yourself.

- ½ cup lilac petals
- 2 teaspoons lavender flowers
- 2 teaspoons pennyroyal
- 1 white rose (white is the color of peace)
- Sweetener to taste
- 1 teaspoon violet petals, chopped
- 1½ cups carbonated water (seltzer)

Simmer your flowers in just enough plain water so the petals are covered. Wait until the petals turn translucent, gently squeeze the petals into the water, then add the carbonated water and sweetener to taste. By the way, without the carbonated water, this makes a lovely magical finger bowl to inspire gentle writing (for letters), kind handshakes, and for dipping into just before a long, hand-in-hand walk with your lover.

Alternative Ingredients: If this is being prepared to bring peace to a struggling relationship, I'd suggest changing to a red rose. Also, if you're not a big fan of flowers, you can use one cup of warm apple juice with a fresh sprig of mint to achieve the same results.

Other Magical Uses: Try dabbing a bit of this in any room or area where there's been a lot of anger or tension as you recite an incantation or focus on peaceful energies filling the air.

Yields 1½ to 2 cups.

WISH TONIC
For manifestation, new beginnings,
bountiful success

History and Folklore: Daisies and dandelions have long been used in magical wishing customs. Clover brings luck, pansy restores hope, honey attracts life's sweetness, and sage balances our hopes and dreams with a little wisdom.

- 1 teaspoon dried clover flowers
- Petals from one daisy, one pansy, and one dandelion
- 1 cinnamon stick
- ¼ teaspoon sage
- 1 cup hot water
- Honey to taste

Put the petals, clover flowers, and sage into a tea ball or gauze bundle and steep in the hot water until the tea is heady with aroma. Stir in the honey clockwise to generate positive energy, focusing on your wishes as you do. Stir with a cinnamon stick.

Alternative Ingredients: If your wish centers around personal health, use apple and/or orange tea instead of the flowers and petals. Stir with a stick of cinnamon for increased power.

Other Magical Uses: Carry the dried, blessed components in a container with you. Then, when a wish comes up, scatter the petals to the winds so they can carry your desire to all of creation.

Yields 1 cup.

Foods

The foods that can potentially come out of a Green Witch's garden are fairly diverse, ranging from fruity desserts and marinades, herbal vinegars, and spicy oils, to vegetable-laden appetizers, entrees, soups, and side dishes. Needless to say, this made choosing recipes for this section somewhat difficult. So, like any good Green Witch, I simply relied on creativity and my personal pallet to guide me. Please don't let the limited nature of this selection hold you back, however. Any dish can become a magical masterpiece if you have the will and focus necessary to spark energy toward your goal.

MYSTIC MUSHROOMS
FOR PSYCHIC AWARENESS, FAIRY FRIENDSHIP, TRANQUILITY

HISTORY AND FOLKLORE: Egyptians regarded mushrooms as food for the gods, while Romans consumed them for physical vitality. The Chinese believed that mushrooms only grow when peace falls across the land, and in Europe, a ring of mushrooms is the fabled home for fairy folk.

NOTE: It's very important that you're careful about what kind of mushrooms you grow! and/or harvest, as some can be deadly. If you're not sure about what you've got, don't use it. Go buy some at the market instead. Also, never pick the mushrooms from a "fairy ring" if you're using this food to improve your rapport with the earth spirits! Such an action is considered rather forward, and pretty insulting to those spirits, so it doesn't make a good impression.

- 1 large portobello or shiitake mushroom per person
- Strawberry-apple juice (to cover the mushrooms)
- 1 tablespoon red wine vinegar per mushroom
- 1 teaspoon thyme
- 1 teaspoon garlic
- 1 teaspoon rosewater
- 1 cup crushed strawberries
- 1 cup honey
- 1 tablespoon crushed garlic

Marinate the mushrooms overnight in the refrigerator using the juice, vinegar, thyme, garlic, and rosewater. When you're ready to grill the next day, in a separate bowl, mix the crushed strawberries, honey, and garlic to use as a baste. Grill mushrooms and turn every 2–3 minutes; remove from the fire after the second turn so the mushrooms don't overcook.

ALTERNATIVE INGREDIENTS: I've found that mushrooms are very versatile. You can marinate them in orange juice and grill them for improved intuitiveness in your relationships, or spice them with onion for psychic protection. Nearly any marinade you use for meat can be easily absorbed into the mushroom's pores, making for very flavorful results.

OTHER MAGICAL USES: Since the head of the mushroom is a natural circle, you can gently carve images of your goal into the surface using a toothpick. Then the circle of protection surrounds your magical work as the heat adds energy to the effort.

Yields 1 serving.

ENCHANTING EGGPLANT
FOR LOVE, ALL TYPES; PASSION

HISTORY AND FOLKLORE: In Moorish tradition, the eggplant was considered an aphrodisiac, and even called a "love apple." In the Middle East, people ate so much eggplant that cookbooks listed over 1,000 ways to prepare this vegetable. Japanese legends also tell us that eggplant, applied to one's teeth, will whiten and brighten them. This, in turn, makes us more alluring to prospective mates.

Anyone who has ever grown eggplant knows you always get too much of it and have to find creative ways to put the extra to use. This particular recipe is one such way. It originates in Turkey where the blend is considered such a delight as to make people swoon. It serves two people, and might best be served by candlelight to increase the romantic ambiance.

- 1 medium eggplant
- ¼ cup olive oil
- 1 teaspoon garlic, crushed
- 1 onion, diced
- 1 large tomato, chopped
- 1 teaspoon oregano (optional)
- Pinch sugar
- Salt and pepper to taste
- 1 teaspoon tomato puree
- 1 tablespoon pine nuts
- ¼ cup seasoned breadcrumbs
- Parmesan cheese (optional)
- Parsley (optional)

Poach the eggplant whole for about 15 minutes then cool in a basin of cold water. Next, cut the eggplant in half lengthwise. Scoop out the pulp, keeping it aside, leaving a little to support the eggplant's skin. Dab the inside and outside of the halves with olive oil (you can season the oil if you wish). Put these in a nonstick baking dish, open side up.

FILLING: Begin by gently sautéing the garlic and onion in the remaining olive oil. Add the tomato, oregano, sugar, and salt or pepper to taste. Cook over a low flame for 15–20 minutes, stirring occasionally. Finally, add the pine nuts, tomato paste, and breadcrumbs. Mix well, then stuff both halves of the shell. Cover and bake at 350°F for 20 minutes. Uncover and bake for an additional 10 minutes. Garnish with freshly grated Parmesan cheese and a sprig of parsley to sweeten your breath for kissability afterward.

ALTERNATIVE INGREDIENTS: If you're not fond of pine nuts, you can use slivered almonds or pistachios. Also, you can add a smoky cheese to this dish (without nuts) to increase the warm emotions it evokes.

OTHER MAGICAL USES: I must confess that I'm not a big eggplant fan, so rather than eating it, I sometimes use it in wish magic. For this, slice the eggplant in half and put something biodegradable in the middle that represents your wish. Bury the halves in the ground. By the time the eggplant completely returns to the soil, your wish should manifest itself.

Yields 2 servings.

MANIFESTATION PUFF
FOR VARIOUS USES, ACCORDING
TO THE VEGETABLE USED

HISTORY AND FOLKLORE: A lot depends on what vegetable you choose from your garden to be the keynote of this dish. A cauliflower, for example, was associated with lunar energy because it looks like the Moon, being white in color and of a similar shape (note the law of Similars and Sympathy). Bearing this correspondence in mind, the resulting recipe would "lift" one's intuitive nature to a higher level. Spinach, thanks to its green leafy nature, is a perfect vehicle for prosperity puffs; a blend of carrots and asparagus augments passion; and an olive and onion blend safeguards peace.

- 3 cups vegetable(s), diced
- ¼ cup butter
- 2 tablespoons flour
- 1 cup milk or half-and-half
- Seasonings to taste
- ¼ cup Italian-style bread crumbs
- 3 eggs, separated
- 1 cup grated cheese Parmesan cheese (optional)

Wash and dice your chosen vegetable(s), steam or precook in boiling water until tender, and drain. Next, warm the butter in a pan, adding the flour to make a paste. Turn off the flame and add the milk slowly, stirring constantly. When this is smooth, turn the burner back on, adding seasonings and breadcrumbs. Gently stir in the egg yolks and some grated cheese to the vegetables. Set aside while you beat the egg whites to fluffy. Fold this into the vegetable mix. Put the entire blend into a greased quart-sized dish. Sprinkle with the remaining grated cheese and bake at 400° F for 30 minutes or until golden brown and puffy.

ALTERNATIVE INGREDIENTS: Choose your spices so they match your goals more specifically. Also, potatoes can be used in this dish for foundations or health, and mushrooms can be added for psychic awareness.

OTHER MAGICAL USES: Anything that you place in the center of a puff will receive uplifting energy. So, if you want to take a cookie that looks like you and bake it in the middle of the puff when your spirits are low, go for it! Eat the cookie to internalize the energy. Marjoram would be the ideal spice to aid this particular magical theme.

Yields 2 servings (as a side dish).

PEACE PORRIDGE
FOR HARMONY, UNITY, ACCORD, TRANQUILITY

HISTORY AND FOLKLORE: Roses, especially the white ones, are considered an emblem of peace and trust. Cumin augments the same energy with tranquil energies. This particular recipe originates in Germany and could be readily found in early twentieth-century cookbooks. It's high in vitamin C, so it improves the overall health of a person or a relationship, too!

- ½ pound fresh or dried rose hips
- Pinch of cumin
- 6 cups water
- 2 ounces flour
- 3 tablespoons sherry
- ¼ cup blanched, shredded almonds
- 1 teaspoon lemon juice
- 1 tablespoon sugar Cream (optional)
- Dumplings (optional)

Rinse the rose hips and simmer with cumin in the water until tender. Pour mixture through a strainer or sieve. Place the rose hips back in a pot and add the remaining ingredients, using the flour as a thickening agent (cornstarch will work too). When the porridge has a pleasant consistency, serve with a garnish of sweet cream or dumplings.

ALTERNATIVE INGREDIENTS: Violets and lavender are two other edible petals that could be added to this porridge. Mint, marjoram, or oregano are alternatives for cumin. If you wish to retain the same energies but make the recipe with a vegetable, I'd suggest two large cucumbers (substituting white wine for the sherry and milk for the water).

OTHER MAGICAL USES: Save a few of the rose hips before cooking and toss them to the winds with an incantation that expresses your wish for peace. Or, you can candy a few of the almonds and carry them with you, eating them when you need a little sweet tranquility.

Yields 2–4 servings.

Oils, Vinegars, Marinades, and Sauces

For readers who are not vegetarian, and who would like to use their Green Witch's garden for making meat more magical, this section will round out your favorite recipes with flavor and positive energy. For vegetarians, you'll find the oils, sauces, and vinegars here are equally good on greens with little, if any, adjustment.

SOLAR OIL
FOR CONSCIOUS MIND, LEADERSHIP, COURAGE, STRENGTH, AND BLESSING

HISTORY AND FOLKLORE: Bay was saved by Apollo, the sun god, making it an ideal ingredient to honor the solar disk.

- 2 cups olive oil*
- 4 good-sized bay leaves
- 2 teaspoons fresh rosemary

* Olive oil has a long shelf life and is a good, all-purpose kitchen oil. However, other types can be considered for their flavor or magical correspondences. In particular, I like almond oil for its flavor and texture. Magically, this accents prosperity, love, and wisdom; sesame oil improves passion; saffron oil promotes joy, strength, and psychic awareness; and corn oil motivates luck.

Warm the oil over a low flame in a non-aluminum pot. Steep the rosemary and bay leaves until the oil has a strong aroma. Strain and store in an airtight container. If the oil turns cloudy at any time, discard. This means the oil has "turned" which also destroys the magical qualities.

ALTERNATIVE INGREDIENTS: Another Asian-oriented solar blend would be sesame, sunflower, and cashew. Or try chrysanthemum petals, marigold, and a hint of orange. An alternative is to substitute lunar flowers and plants for solar ones to make a cooking oil that accents the subconscious, intuitive spirit. In particular, lemon balm oil or wintergreen oil are good choices.

OTHER MAGICAL USES: Once an oil is completed, depending on the base you use, there are a lot of other ways to use it in magic other than for cooking: rub some into your altar tools; dab it on windowsills or doorways for protection and blessing; smear a bit on a particular chakra to open the pathway for spiritual energy; or, bottle an assortment and give it to a friend who shares your metaphysical outlook!

Yields 2 cups.

BLOSSOMING VINEGAR
FOR BANISHING AND PSYCHIC PROTECTION

HISTORY AND FOLKLORE: Vinegar, by its acidic nature, has a protective quality and each of the flowers included in this recipe has been traditionally used for exorcism, hex breaking, and safety.

- 2 teaspoons fresh sage blossoms
- 1 teaspoon fresh rosemary flowers
- White wine vinegar (enough to cover flowers)
- Salt, pepper, or sugar to taste (optional)
- ½ cup each clover, lilac, peony, chrysanthemum, and geranium petals

Warm the vinegar over low heat and pour it into a jar with a large mouth into which the flowers are placed. Add the remaining ingredients and shake thoroughly. Leave this in a sunny window for one to two days, shaking regularly until the flower petals turn translucent. Strain and transfer into a dark bottle with an airtight top. This should last for 6–10 months (throw it away if it turns cloudy). This is quite tasty on green salads, especially those containing fresh flower petals as an ingredient.

ALTERNATIVE INGREDIENTS: Rather than making your vinegar with flowers, you could use thematic herbs instead (this is especially nice for marinades or salad dressings). For protection, use basil, bay, garlic, and sage. For health, try garlic, mint, and thyme.

Yields 2 to 2½ cups.

BERRY ABUNDANCE MARINADE
FOR HAPPINESS, PROSPERITY, AND BOUNTY

HISTORY AND FOLKLORE: Berries have always been considered a symbol of the Earth's abundance, and consequently have been used to inspire abundance in life. Exactly what kind of abundance can vary by the berry type. Blueberries inspire peace with their color, blackberries improve financial foundations, mulberries bring wisdom and intuitiveness, and both raspberries and strawberries inspire joy and love. This particular marinade magically augments any food prepared for happy, well-balanced relationships, with a little ginger added in for passionate "spice" and positive energy.

- ¼ cup each raspberries, strawberries, and blackberries
- ½ cup wine vinegar
- 1 teaspoon powdered ginger
- 1 teaspoon sugar (optional)

Mix the berries together and gently crush them, retaining all the juices. Add vinegar, ginger, and sugar. Stir well. Pour the entire mixture over the intended meat or vegetable (it's particularly good on chicken and sweet potatoes). Refrigerate for 12 hours, then cook using the marinade as a baste.

ALTERNATIVE INGREDIENTS: If you wish to safeguard a relationship, add some garlic or onion powder to the marinade. For greater passion, use cinnamon, mint, celery seed, or a bit of vanilla extract.

OTHER MAGICAL USES: Use this vinegar to baste various meats and vegetables or as part of a berry-based salad dressing when combined with oil.

Yields 1½ cup.

YIN-YANG SAUCE
FOR BALANCING THE GOD AND GODDESS;
SUN AND MOON

HISTORY AND FOLKLORE: This sauce originates in China where the concept of yin-yang energies (and flavors) complementing one another was well-known and often explored in the kitchen by healers and common folk alike. In this particular recipe, we have the cool sweetness of sugar, carrots, and bamboo against the hot sourness of garlic, scallions, ginger, and vinegar.

- ¼ cup peanut oil
- 2 cloves garlic, minced
- 4 scallions, diced
- 1 small carrot, chopped
- 1 tablespoon cornstarch
- ½ cup brown sugar
- 2 teaspoons powdered ginger
- 2 tablespoons white vinegar
- 3 tablespoons soy sauce
- ¼ cup bamboo shoots, sliced
- ¼ cup water chestnuts, sliced
- 1½ cups chicken broth

Sauté the garlic in the peanut oil until lightly browned. Add the scallions and carrots, continuing to stir for about 3 minutes. Mix in the sugar, ginger, vinegar, and soy sauce, simmering for 2–3 minutes more. In a separate bowl, blend the cornstarch with the chicken broth and pour over vegetables. Stir until thickened. Add the water chestnuts and bamboo shoots just prior to serving.

ALTERNATIVE INGREDIENTS: Many people enjoy adding pineapple (for hospitality) or mandarin oranges (luck, love, or prosperity) to this recipe for a little more sweetness and color.

OTHER MAGICAL USES: Pour a little over rice for slow improvements in providence, use it as a glaze on meats for securing finances, or use specifically on pork for spiritual balance.

Yields 1½ cups.

ROMANTIC SAUCE
FOR IMPROVING RELATIONSHIPS,
FRIENDSHIPS, OR SELF-LOVE

HISTORY AND FOLKLORE: Among Italians, this sauce is a classic, and it is still made by the elders of the community to help bring star-crossed lovers together. The tomato, the base of this sauce, is often called a love apple. The herbs accent good feelings and positive energy.

- 2 tablespoons olive oil
- 2 tablespoons butter
- 1 large green onion, diced
- 2 cloves garlic, chopped
- 1 small green pepper, diced
- 1 bay leaf
- ½ cup beef stock

- 4 cups fresh tomatoes, chopped
- 1 teaspoon each basil, chives, oregano, and rosemary
- 1 teaspoon sugar
- ½ teaspoon tomato paste

Sauté the onion, garlic, green pepper, bay leaf, and tomato in olive oil and butter until tender. Add the beef stock, herbs, tomatoes, and sugar and simmer slowly for one hour. Remove the bay leaf and strain the sauce. Return the sauce to the stove and add the tomato paste for thickening and texture. Serve over pasta or toasted bread with grated cheese.

ALTERNATIVE INGREDIENTS: You can add meat or eggplant to the sauce for more body. Also, eggplant accentuates love, while meat provides a solid foundation and prosperity. Other herbs sometimes included are parsley and thyme.

OTHER MAGICAL USES: The garlic and onions in this recipe make it good for protection. Also, the red coloration means that this sauce can be used as a substitute for blood in older spells.

Yields 5 cups.

Other Goodies

There are obviously a lot more recipes than I could cover in just this material due to space constraints. For example, how about a nice summer harvest salad with edible petals as a garnish? Blend in some sesame dressing and you've got a healthy side dish charged with energy for financial abundance. Or, how about just nibbling a fresh-picked cucumber for devotion or fertility; a couple of peas (in the pod) to help in your quest to find a soul mate; or a couple of raspberries dunked in ginger ale to increase happiness? These are simple, yet sumptuous ways to enjoy the energy and flavor of everything you grow, and even things you don't! Since nearly every meal has some kind of culinary spice included in it, discover the magical meaning already present and weave the energy into your food. It need not be any more complex than that—thoughtfulness, a little willpower, and a lot of Green Witchery! For more ideas like this, check out my book, *A Kitchen Witch's Cookbook*.

Chapter 5

Aromatic Magic and Handcrafts

*"The scent of flowers comes and goes
like the warbling of music."*
—Francis Bacon

One cannot walk through a field of flowers without noticing the fragrance that fills the air (unless, of course, you have allergies!), or the beauty that surrounds you. Even those who disdain the pollen season often find themselves taken with the amazing aroma and appeal of newly-opened blossoms or freshly harvested herbs. It tickles our senses physically and psychically, which is also what makes aromatics a wonderful vehicle for Green Witchcraft.

As the scent of a bouquet wafts through the air, it carries a specific energy signature with it. As our minds interpret the things we see, that also creates energy. This means that a Green Witch can experience the metaphysical vibrations of flowers and plants on a sensual and rather intimate level. Think for a moment of how you feel when you smell bread baking, and imagine it just as it pops out of the oven. I personally find my mouth watering in anticipation.

This isn't a reaction I *try* to create; it's quite automatic. Similarly, the reaction our bodies, minds, and spirits experience with magically charged sights and smells can be quite startling and effortless, but for the willpower and time you put into making them.

The purpose behind this material, therefore, is twofold. The first is to give you some more ways of using those items grown in the Green Witch's garden (or those that have been properly blessed from other sources). The second is to give you some crafty vehicles for magic that also have a subtle, spiritual appeal (meaning they don't scream "Witch" to any overly curious onlookers).

Air Fresheners

Think about the name of this product for just a moment. Air freshener: In those two words, we have some great hints for applying this item magically. First, and most obvious, is honoring or working with the Air element. In this case, you'll want to create a blend that includes Air flowers, spices, or plant parts such as lavender, lemongrass, or mint. As you blend these, add an incantation, such as:

> *"Spirit of the four winds, empower this simple blend, that with each use it will bear the attributes of sacred Air!"*

Second comes "freshener." What is it in your life or home that needs to be refreshed? Say your zest for life has been lagging lately. I would recommend using a blend that accentuates youthful enthusiasm and energy like rosemary, carnation, and myrtle. In this case, the incantation might take this form:

> *"Rosemary for youth, carnation for zeal, myrtle for my body and mind to heal. When from my hand these herbs pour, let personal energy be restored!"*

This is nice in that it keys the effect of the air freshener to when you release it (meaning it's inert between uses).

Mind you, there isn't anything that says you can't create air fresheners for any magical purpose you desire, especially those goals that work cooperatively with the wind's attributes (these include: liberation, movement, luck, psychic awareness, and imagination). For example, if you need to improve communication in your home, make an air freshener with ingredients like rosemary, sage, and lilac, adding an incantation like:

"Words be sweet, anger abate, help our family communicate!"

There are three different kinds of air fresheners that I make: wax-based, potpourri, and carpet powders.

WAX FRESHENER: To make a wax-based freshener, begin by melting about 1 cup of solid paraffin or candle wax in a pan over low heat. Once it reaches a liquid stage, add the base aromatic(s) that you've chosen. I suggest you make this rather potent as the aroma will diminish upon cooling, and it needs to be strong to have a long shelf life. You can alternatively use finely powdered herbs, but I've found that oils are far more effective.

Once the aromatics are integrated, let the wax cool to the point where you can handle it (it will have a tacky or doughy consistency). You can now knead it into a ball (or any other shape desired) around a loop of string. Just make sure the string is well secured in the wax. Let this completely harden, then hang it in a sunny window or over a warm area (heater outlet, stove, etc., but be careful it's not near enough to melt and drip!). When the wax has no more aroma, you can use it as a candle or melt it down again and refresh the scent.

POTPOURRI: This is also fast and easy to make. In this case, you'll want to use dried or pressed plant parts (fresh ones will wilt or get moldy). Mix and mingle the chosen components for a pleasant aroma, visual impact, and textural variety. In terms of magic, don't forget to use color symbolism in the blends—like a predominantly green potpourri for prosperity. Use a little food coloring, if need be, to get the right hue. And, as with the wax freshener, remember to mingle your aromas so they have a theme. Returning to the example of prosperity, choices include basil, chamomile, honeysuckle, mint, and pine, which combine nicely with this incantation:

"Blessed basil, money mint, prosperity pine, within your scents let magic shine, and soon abundance will be mine!"

CARPET FRESHENER: This form of freshener is great for homes with pets or children. I make mine using a baking soda base because of its natural cleansing qualities, but you can use orris root powder instead. In any case, the basic formula is six parts baking soda, one part finely powdered herb, and an added essential oil as desired. Mix well. Once this is thoroughly mixed, you *must* let the carpet powder dry completely and sift it before using. This keeps the essential oil from staining the rug and ensures that the blend vacuums up easily.

Don't forget to chant or incant as you vacuum since this machine can symbolically "suck up" negativity. Something like *"Sadness and negativity drawn away, only good energy is here to stay"* might be fitting. Maybe work through your house counterclockwise for banishing, or sweep from the center of the room outwards to move any bad vibes away from the heart of the home.

Beads

Generally, the beads in the following recipe are created from flower petals, but a little experimentation can yield positive results with aromatic leaves or barks, too. The basic process is as follows:

1. Gather the desired plant parts and dice them really small. Using only one type of flora works best, but I have had some success with blends.

2.   Put the pieces in a blender or food processor and puree, adding just enough water to get a very fine texture.

3.   Pour this blend into an iron pot and simmer for an hour. Repeat steps 2 and 3 until the resulting plant matter is pasty.

4.   Add a few drops of essential oil to the mixture (or separate parts and scent each one differently). You can also add food coloring at this juncture for magical symbolism and personal appeal.

5.   Form the beads as large or small as you like. Bear in mind that they will shrink around 30–50 percent during drying.

6.   String the beads on thread, yarn, or twine. Your choice of string depends on what size hole you'd like to have in the finished beads.

7.   Turn the beads daily so that they dry evenly, and that the diameter of the hole is likewise symmetrical. As you do, sing to the beads or speak spells over them to saturate the finished product with energy that reflects their ultimate purpose.

Beads take about three weeks to dry completely, after which you can sew them onto your magical robes; add them to potpourri; toss them into hampers to charge your clothes with energy; or string them for prayer beads, necklaces, or earrings. In making any of the last three, remember to choose your components accordingly, like roses for Goddess-oriented prayers, a necklace of violet beads to safeguard your words, and maybe earrings from clove to offset a tendency to listen to gossip.

Bookmarks

By far the easiest way to make bookmarks is out of sturdy paper, like the kind used for greeting cards. Cut out an image or shape that represents your goal. Dab this with a corresponding oil. The result will be a bookmark that doubles as aromatherapy while you study your Book of Shadows, spells, or rituals!

NOTE: This works on larger pieces of paper too, so that you can add a magical signature to any letter or note you send!

A more complex version can be created as follows:

1. Begin with sturdy paper (found at any craft store).

2. Apply pressed flower petals and leaves. I suggest placing these on the surface of the paper without glue at first so you can move them if you don't like the way they look.

3. Once you achieve an eye-pleasing pattern, secure each piece with durable adhesive. Let this dry.

4. Dab each flower or herb with a corresponding essential oil, also letting this dry.

5. Cover the entire bookmark with a protective coating (like lamination).

For the magical dimension, don't forget that you can make different bookmarks that visually and sensually augment the energies of different books or book sections. For example, you might keep a rosemary bookmark in the part of a resource book that you want to memorize. Or, you might place a rose bookmark in the section of your Book of Shadows that talks about love spells and rituals.

Candles

Can you imagine Witches without candles? Candles are nearly indispensable tools, and for the Green Witch, they represent another way to put nature's aromas and beauties to work.

The easiest way to make your own candles is by using molds, wicks, and wax purchased at a hobby shop or craft store. To save a little money, you can use household items for molds like old milk cartons, or oiled muffin dishes and gelatin containers. The oil makes it much easier to release the candle from the mold once the wax cools. Once you have the necessary ingredients, follow this process:

1. Before you melt the wax, consider whether you want to place any flowers or plant parts in the bottom of the mold. If you do, the chosen item should symbolize the foundation of your magical goal. For example, a love candle might be constructed on top of an elder leaf so the relationship has fidelity at its base, providing support and strength.

2. Next, you'll want to decide what type of scent to add to your candle. Essential oils are a very easy option because they don't require any special preparation and yet have strong aromas. You won't need a lot to bring a gentle fragrance to the wax, but it's a good idea to add just a little extra for longevity.

3. An alternative way to scent your candles is to add finely ground, dried plant parts. I say *dried* because anything fresh tends to (a) gather mold, (b) decompose, or (c) spark when flame touches it because of small water particles within. The amount and variety of dried herbs and flowers that you add really depends on personal taste. I find that about 2–3 tablespoons added to a quart milk carton candle is a nice touch

without being overwhelming. Also, too much dried material can hinder the stability of your finished candle while it burns (parts could fall off and ruin wood or cloth surfaces, or worse—cause a fire). To avoid this, it helps to sift your dried components before adding them to the melted wax. Also, make sure these components are evenly dispersed in the wax.

4.   Melt the wax in a double boiler and add the components you've chosen. Pour this into the mold. Let cool completely.

5.   Release the candle from its mold by running a little hot water over the outside.

6.   Consider if you'd like to add some more plant parts as magical decoration on the outside of the candle. Returning to our previous example of love, some waxed elder leaves or flowers might be attached to the candle at the bottom using small dabs of melted wax as a glue. A health candle might have pressed morning glories around it to promote happiness, which is essential to emotional and spiritual well-being. Note, too, that since a Green Witch works equally well with other citizens of the natural world, they might also choose to decorate the candle with small crystals to improve its visual appeal and overall energy.

For those of you wishing to scent premade candles, essential oils and pantry spices are both great. Simply line a box with a cotton cloth. Sprinkle your chosen oil or spice over the cloth, folding the cloth inward toward the middle of the box so the aromatic doesn't come into direct contact with the wax. Store your candles covered, and they will slowly absorb some of the fragrance (perhaps leave them for a year and a day, in a cool location, corresponding to the traditional study time of a Witch before initiation).

Alternatively, anoint the candles before using them instead. In either case, your essential oil should be chosen for its mystical significance to you, and cleansed beforehand unless you've made your own (see later in this section). After all, you don't know who bottled these oils or what their mindset was at that moment. Magic always flows best through a spiritually clean vehicle, and cleansing or blessing are the extra steps that create that purified vehicle.

If you're uncertain of how to clean or bless the oil, here are two suggestions:

- Pass the bottle through the smoke of a purifying incense like sage, then say a prayer over it by way of blessing and empowering the oil for its intended use.
- Hold your hands palm-down over the bottle. Close your eyes, take a deep breath, and visualize the entire bottle being filled with a brilliant white light. To this process, add a brief incantation like *"Blessings, and goodness, and light—all negativity take flight!"*

HINT: Have any bits and pieces of incense around the house? Grind these up and add them to the melted wax! It's a great way to recycle, save time, scent the candle, and mix in some magic.

The Green Witch need not stop with the symbolic value of their candle's aroma, however. Consider sprinkling a little glitter into the wax to give the visual appearance of magic being afoot, or add symbolic sparkle. Cut your candles into magical shapes like a square for an Earth-oriented candle, or a triangle to accent the triune nature. You can smooth off rough edges using a cloth laid over top and gently press with a warm iron. Really, the options are nearly endless.

By the way, remember the Green Witch's ideal of reusing anything we can as a way of recycling and being careful with Earth's resources? Well, save your candle remnants in boxes or bags, labeled, and sorted by magical theme. This way, you can remelt the wax later to make new candles. Better still, these remnants already bear the energy signature from the first molding and are saturated with energy from the magical process(es) for which you used them. So, the finished, recycled candles will have even more latent power just waiting to be activated!

Headpieces

Many magical practitioners like to wear a crown of flowers or aromatic herbs for festivals and gatherings. It's a lovely addition to the overall costume and has symbolic value besides. However, natural headpieces take a little patience to fashion effectively.

For those people lacking in plentiful spare time, those who don't regard themselves as very coordinated (that's me), or those who want a finished headpiece that will last, I suggest weaving a crown out of silk flowers and dabbing them with essential oil rather than using fresh plants. Most silk flowers are made on a stem of flexible metal wire or bendable plastic, so they'll be very easy to connect. The only caution is to make sure you don't leave any rough edges exposed. These can cause scratches and cuts. A decorative solution is to wrap the completed headpiece with a ribbon between each flower or leaf.

Readers who want to try the fresh approach can follow these guidelines:

1. Pick leaves and/or flowers with long, pliable stems.

2. Tie a loose knot just below the flower or leaf base.

3. Thread the next stem through the knot so that the flower or leaf faces forward just below the first one.

4. Repeat steps 2 and 3 until the chain is long enough to tie off at the end.

5.   Use a decorative ribbon to complete the look, twining it in and out of the flowers or leaves and allowing the extra to hang down the back of your head.

If you cannot find leaves with long enough stems to knot, another way to connect them is to simply push the stem of the first leaf down through the top of the second. Turn this upward again (as if you were sewing) and put the stem through the first leaf from the bottom up. Perhaps add an incantation like *"Leaves that join each to each, so the magic will never cease! Nature power here is bound, as the circle comes around."*

Be aware that this particular configuration isn't overly secure, so the addition of a ribbon will help a lot. Or, you can add a dab of glue to keep the chain "connected" and let it dry before finishing off the ends.

Incense

Most of the incense recipes I've found include ingredients that aren't overly conducive to magic, however, they do allow the incense to burn without a fire source (such as the sticks and cones you can buy commercially). Honestly, I see nothing wrong with a Green Witch purchasing their incense ready-made since it's a great time-saver. My only precaution is to remember to bless and charge the product for its intended use.

If you're unfamiliar with blessing and charging items, it's very easy to learn how. A blessing usually takes the form of a prayer where you indicate the intended use for the item and ask your God/dess (or universal powers) to ordain and consecrate the item for that purpose. Charging simply activates the latent energy in an item through visualization or ritualistic actions. A common visualization is of pure white light filling the components. Actions include leaving the item in the light of the sun (for the conscious mind and Fire/Air energy) or the moonlight (for the intuitive nature or Water/Earth energy) for a symbolic number of hours or days. Sometimes, phases of the moon are added to this equation, like letting a component charge by the light of a waning moon so it will work effectively in banishing magic.

If you wish to make incense yourself, it can be very satisfying and spiritually fulfilling. The type that requires an active fire source is wholly organic. It begins with a cup of sandalwood powder to which you add finely ground herbs, plants, and oils. Be sure to mix this thoroughly, sift it, then let it dry before storing in an airtight container. Use no more than three additional ingredients for best results and test the blend on a fire to be sure you like the aroma when it burns (the way it smells dry can be quite different).

For a self-burning cone incense:

1. You'll need 4 parts sandalwood powder, 20 parts finely dried herbs, and 1 part gum arabic.

2. To this, you'll need to add ¼ cup of water mixed with ¼ cup of saltpeter for every 25 teaspoons of dried mix.

3. Slowly stir in the liquid until you achieve a dough-like texture. Form into cones.

4. Put the finished cone on waxed paper to dry. It will take three to four days before these are ready to store or use, depending on surrounding humidity levels.

Again, don't overlook the opportunity to use magical processes while you make your incense. Chant, incant, stir clockwise (positive energy) or counterclockwise (banishing or turning energy), add symbolic coloring, and so forth. This way the finished product will produce the desired effects, as well as lovely aromas.

Notepaper

You can scent your stationery using essential oils or dried spices, but you can also make your own paper from scratch using Green Witch ingenuity as a helpmate. Here's how:

1. Fashion some frames from old coat hangers. The frames need not necessarily be square unless you want Earthy energy. Make round ones for lunar/Water influences, triangular ones for the body/mind/spirit connection, and so forth. Stretch pantyhose over the frame so it acts like a strainer. You'll want about 4 or 5 frames in total.

2. Gather the following items: scrap paper that equals at least 4 newspaper pages, a blender, a bottle of school glue, and enough water to cover the newspaper. Make sure you have access to a sink with a stopper, or at least a large wash basin, in which to strain the sheets of paper.

3. Take about a quarter of the scrap paper and rip it into tiny pieces. Put this in the blender and pulp it using a little of the water. Set this batch aside and repeat with the rest of the paper until it's all pulped.

4. When all the paper is pulped, put the entire batch in the blender for about 3 minutes, adding finely powdered dry herbs, oils, food coloring, glitter, ribbon, or other personal touches to make the paper truly unique and personally pleasing. Other optional ingredients include feathers, lace, scrap threads, tea, coffee, chopped flowers, and confetti.

5. Fill the sink with 6 inches of water. Place your frames at the bottom.

6. Pour the pulped paper into the water along with 4 tablespoons of glue. Mix well.

7. Slowly lift the first frame through the water so it collects the fibers evenly. Repeat with the remaining frames.

8. Store any leftover pulp in a covered container in the refrigerator for up to a week if you want to make more paper.

9. Remove the liquid from the sink and pour it outside if possible. The glue and small paper bits may clog your drains.

10. Dry each frame completely. I suggest hanging them on a clothesline, either outside or over your tub, as they will drip.

11. Gently tap the back of the frame to release the sheet.

12. Put each sheet on the ironing board, cover it with a kitchen towel, and press with an iron on medium heat. This removes any excess water and provides a smoother writing surface.

13. Finally, leave these open to the air for 72 hours before using them. Store the paper in a scented box to maintain its aromatic appeal and sustain the magic.

Perfumed Oils

Making aromatic oils is one of my favorite pastimes. I enjoy using them in the kitchen, around the house, in my bath, as perfumes, and as gifts. While it takes a little while to become adept at making an aromatic oil, once you develop the knack, it easily applies to any other oils you create.

AROMATIC MAGICK AND HANDCRAFTS

The simplest way to make an aromatic oil is by using a combination base oil to which essentials are added. To every cup of base, you'll likely need about 10 drops of essential oil, but go slowly. Test the blend after 5 drops to see if you like the aroma on your skin. This also ensures that you'll discover any sensitivity you may have long before it becomes a problem. For body oils, I personally prefer almond oil as the base, but some people use good quality, light olive oil instead. Olive oil takes very quickly to aromas and has a long shelf life.

A more time-consuming method for making your oils is steeping:

1.   Begin with one-part dried plant parts, two parts fresh plant parts, and three parts oil.

2.   Warm the oil over a low flame.

3.   Steep your chosen aromatics in the oil until it has a tea-like quality.

4.   Strain and repeat with the resulting oil until you achieve the desired potency.

5.   Store in a dark, airtight container for up to six months.

Two words of caution exist regarding the second method. First, do not boil the oil. Some plants, flowers in particular, are very heat sensitive. If the oil is too hot, the results will be very unpleasant. Second, except in the case of green aromatic herbs (bay), do not allow any leafy plant parts into the steeping process. As the oil ages, the plant parts create a funny smell that's hard to describe, but it somewhat resembles old sweat socks! If you avoid these two pitfalls, your efforts should prove successful.

Signature Scents

One really fun thing to do with aromatic oils is to create magical signature scents for yourself and your friends. You can base this on a predominant personality trait, a spiritual focus, an element, or whatever. For example, as a Kitchen Witch, I created an oil for myself out of my favorite pantry spices: cinnamon, vanilla, ginger, orange powder, and so on. This smells a lot like cookies, and it's just perfect for those times when I'm doing spellcraft at the stove. Another example is the oil I made for a friend. She has a strong Water element in her personality so I blended lemon balm, heather, violet, thyme, and vanilla for her.

In making signature scents, one item becomes what's called a *keynote*. The other components of the oil uplift, augment, and flatter this keynote in various ways (by making it sweeter, spicier, mellower, etc.). A good example is rose, which is a keynote for many floral blends. To this foundation a lot of other flowers or spices might be added, rounding out the aroma.

Taking this idea one step further, everything in the temporal world has an astral presence, including an oil's keynote. So, you can use this concept to boost magical energy. In this case, the keynote component of your oil should represent the energy you're trying to create or bear the right vibration to support the entire blend with strength and symmetry.

CREAM VERSION

I have several friends who don't like the feel of oil or who have such oily skin that wearing this kind of product is uncomfortable. Turning the oil into a cream is the perfect solution. It also combines two different products from this material: your homemade candles and oils.

The basic proportions for skin cream are half-and-half (equal parts melted wax to oil). To this base, you can add essential oils or emulsifying herbs. Note that you can substitute cocoa butter or coconut oil for wax, since both harden when cooled, and both effectively condition the skin. Once you've gathered your ingredients (wax, herbs, oils, etc.), follow this process:

1. Melt the wax, cocoa butter, or coconut oil over a low flame until completely liquified.

2. Add the essential oils and emulsifying herbs.

3. Remove from the stove. As the blend cools, you'll need to beat it constantly, I recommend using a whisk or a wooden skewer (the second is disposable and so you won't waste so much of your cream).

4. Continue until the entire blend has reached room temperature and is thoroughly mixed, by which time you should have achieved a cold cream-like texture.

5. Store in an airtight container with an identifying label.

By the way, if the cream starts losing its aroma, you can melt it slightly and add extra essential oil. You can also use it warm as a massage cream that rubs energy right into a person's auric envelope.

Poppet

An old magical tool, poppets are basically handmade dolls filled with herbs and plant parts that represent a goal. Thanks to the re-emergence of folk art, having one or two of these around your home won't be thought of as unusual! And, since you can make these little dolls in any shape, they can work equally well for people and pets.

Now, if you're not an overly adept craftsperson, you can cheat a bit and buy a cloth doll or stuffed animal that resembles the person or creature for whom the magic is intended. Open one of the seams and remove a little stuffing. Replace this with flower petals, spices, and so on that represent your goal.

The alternative is to sew the poppet from two pieces of cloth, leaving open the head to add stuffing and herbs. Then, as you close the final seam, pray or incant a spell and know that your magic is safely within, radiating without.

By the way, those of you who have never worked with poppets before should bear in mind that you can use them for sympathetic magic. For example, if this were a healing poppet, you might want to bury it in the earth so that the sickness is grounded out and moved away from the afflicted. Or, if you make love poppets, these should be stored close together to inspire emotional closeness.

Pot Holder

For this craft project, you'll want to go to a store and find a decorative pot holder whose colors, patterns, or images somehow symbolize your magical goal. For example, if you plan to use this for kitchen magic, you might want to find one that depicts a wooden spoon or something else relating to your sacred pantry.

Once you've got your pot holder, follow these steps:

1. Cut a small square of fabric (2¼ inches by 2¼ inches is good).

   NOTE: Natural fabrics (as opposed to synthetic) are always better for magic.

2. Fold down all four sides of the square about ¼ inch and iron in place.

3. Hand stitch three sides of this to the middle of the back of the oven mitt.

4. Stuff the top of the resulting pocket with whatever herbs and flowers you've chosen, then close up the last side.

5. As you sew, consider adding an incantation like *"As above, so below, fill with magic as I sew!"* Remember to keep the goal of your magic firmly in mind as you recite the incantation.

Hang this off a hook in the kitchen where its aroma can fill the air. Every time you use the mitt in cooking, the heat of the oven will energize and emit your magic.

Sachet and Sweet Bags

Among the crafts of the Green Witch, sachets and sweet bags rank highly for both versatility and ease of creation. These require nothing more than scrap fabric (about 3 inches by 3 inches), a tie (string, yarn, or ribbon), and filling (dried flowers, plants, herbs, fruits, etc.). Now, you can certainly choose a natural fabric of a sympathetic color (something that has a symbolic value, such as green for money), and work during auspicious moon phases, but that's really just icing on the cake.

The key here is putting the components (and the magic) into the center of the fabric, which becomes the nucleus around which energy will rotate. Be careful not to put too much within, or you won't be able to secure the bundle. Then, as you tie the sachet, recite an incantation like:

> *"_____ and _____, bound within, so the magic shall begin. With _____ and _____, my will convey; so within the magic stays!"*

Fill in the first two blanks with words that represent your goal. Fill in the second two blanks with component names, then put the sachet where you most need its energy released slowly (think of this like time-release medication; the magic lasts as long as the sachet's aroma).

Now take the string at the top of the bundle just below the fabric edge and tie a knot. Bear in mind that knot tying is a very old and trusted form of magic wherein you bind energy with the knot. Should you ever need the energy of the sachet to manifest more quickly, untie the bundle and toss the components to the winds. Untying the knot frees your spell, and scattering the contents sends the magic on its way.

By the way, if you ever stumble across small, cotton, draw-string bags in a store, get yourself several. These make very serviceable, reusable sachet/sweet bags, and they don't usually cost a lot.

Dream Pillows

Dream pillows are essentially an over-sized sachet! To make one for yourself, follow these instructions:

1. Cut two equal-sized pieces of fabric, about half an inch larger than you want the finished pillow.

2. Put these two pieces together with their right sides (the one with the pattern or color) facing each other.

3. Half an inch from the edge, sew 3 and a half sides of the pillow. Leave enough space open to insert flowers and herbs. If you are using a sewing machine, you can hand-stitch this final part, saturating the pillow with personal energy. The stuffing can consist of balsam needles, rose petals, hops flowers, marigold petals, lavender flowers, and dried lemon rind (finely powdered). These are all good choices to inspire pleasant and often psychic dreams.

4. Before you stuff it, take a little foam or cotton batting and line the inside of the pillow. Herbs are great for aroma, but they don't make a very comfortable headrest!

5. Fill in this little nest with your chosen components, and possibly a drop or two of aromatic oil for strength and longevity.

6.   Finally, sew up the last seam, adding an incantation like: *"Bring to me blessed dreams; magic stitched in my pillow's seams!"* If the pillow loses its scent, just open up your hand-stitched seam and refresh the components.

Strewing Flowers

In modern times, this old custom is rarely seen but for weddings where a bridesmaid or flower girl sprinkles flower petals in front of the bride. In ancient Greece and Rome, however, it was quite common to toss flowers on the ground during special festivals, as part of celebratory parades, as an expression of adoration during courting, and during specific rituals honoring gods and goddesses. More pragmatically, freshly strewn flower petals helped deter insects and covered up the unpleasant aroma generated by those who were somewhat superstitious about bathing.

Thanks to the wonders of modern appliances that make cleanup so easy, namely vacuum cleaners, we can still use this tradition and apply it to our magic in various ways:

WISHING SPELLS: Gather a handful of flower petals whose aroma, color, or magical correspondences match your goal. Take these outside when the wind is blowing and release them with your wish. Add an incantation if desired, like, "I give these petals to the wind, so the magic can begin. A wish I make, a wish now blessed, let this magic manifest!" The movement of the petals and their scent support the manifestation process.

DIVINATION: Again, choose the petals according to your question. Then strew them on a floor or the surface of some water and watch what patterns emerge. The aromatics in this case help focus your mind on the question.

PROTECTION: Sprinkle flower petals around your sacred space as part of casting the magical circle. Consider using four different types of petals, each of which bears an aroma suited to a specific element (use the Correspondence List) to help with elemental correspondences. One example would be to combine cypress or primrose (Earth), lavender or clover (Air), chrysanthemum or snapdragon (Fire), and violet or periwinkle (Water).

To this process, you'll probably want to add a suitable invocation as you stop at each quarter of the circle, like

"Welcome powers of the East and Air,
I honor you with lavender.

Welcome powers of the South and Sun,
I honor you with snapdragons!

Welcome powers of the West,
who are fertile and wet,
I honor you with violets.

Welcome powers of the North,
whose soils nurture and caress,
I honor you with cypress!"

You can then go to your altar and begin the ritual or whatever function you have planned.

OFFERINGS: Litter the floor of your sacred space with petals that honor your personal God or Goddess.

HANDFASTING OR DEVOTION RITUALS: Since strewn flowers were used in courtship, having something similar present at magical commitments is perfectly apt. Rose is an obvious choice here, as is clover for fidelity.

SACRED DANCING: Have someone in the dance sprinkle flower petals as you move. This creates a lovely aroma throughout the space (magically matching the theme of your gathering), not to mention an inspiring visual effect for the participants.

PATTERN MAGIC: Native Americans and Buddhists use sand to create sacred patterns, generating magic through the process and the imagery. A Green Witch can do this with plants by placing them on the ground in a specific design. For example, a person wishing to explore various aspects of self might create a petaled mandala, then meditate in the center of it. Afterward, the petals can either be released to the Earth or gathered for spellcraft.

Last, but not least, flower petals strewn about the sacred space during spring and summer festivals are a perfect accent that celebrates the Earth's rebirth and bounty. Since these petals will be saturated with positive energy from the festival, participants may wish to collect a few and carry them as charms, or use them later in spells, rituals, and magical handcrafts at home.

Miscellany

Take a walk through your home and note the aromatic products that you use regularly. Consider making those products yourself or adapting them toward your magical goals. Here are just a few ideas for your consideration:

SOAP: Remember how you scented premade candles? This works for unscented soap, too. Consider adding these aromas during propitious moon signs for improved energy. Alternatively, you can whittle unscented soap, add a little water, stir clockwise to generate positive energy, add some symbolic herbs or oils, then remold it. Wash with this soap before rituals, prior to spellcraft or divination efforts, or anytime you want to rub a little magic directly into your aura.

BATH SALTS: This is easy enough. Get some sea salt (strongly aligned with both the Earth and Water elements) and add dried flowers or herbs cut small, and/or essential oils to the blend to suit personal tastes and magical goals. Mix well.

BUTTER AND CREAM CHEESE: Here is another version of edible Green Witchery. Soften the butter or cream cheese then fold in your thematically chosen and magically charged spices. Enjoy!

HAIR RINSE: Basically, you can make a tea to use as a hair rinse out of any flower or herb (and blends thereof) to surround your face with aromatic magic.

INK SECRETS: Elderberry and sloe juice both make serviceable inks. Alternatively, onion juice, lemon juice, or vinegar all dry invisibly to keep the writing in your Book of Shadows private. To reveal the words, simply hold the sheet up to a candle carefully and warm it.

LAUNDRY FRESHENERS: Take a cloth bundle filled with magically enhanced dry herbs and flowers and toss it in the dryer. This will charge your entire wardrobe with power.

See? A Green Witch's domain isn't limited to the outdoors. With a little ingenuity, you can bring that special energy and magic to every part of the house and every part of daily life.

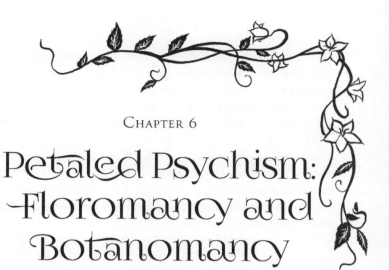

CHAPTER 6

Petaled Psychism: Floromancy and Botanomancy

*"In eastern lands they talk in flowers and tell in a
garland their loves and cares."*
—JAMES G. PERCIVAL

The use of natural objects in divination is widely known
around the world. From the sight of herbs on a crackling fire
to the movements of clouds and birds, humankind has kept
an interested eye on nature for the signs it provides. People
believed that nature was a storehouse of secrets—that all the
mysteries of God and the universe were hidden there if we
knew where to look. So, it's not surprising to discover herbs,
flowers, and other plants and plant parts participating in the
ancient art of fortune-telling, too.

Initially, plants were just watched, like any other part of
nature, for omens. For example, if a myrtle plant blossomed on
someone's doorstep, it portended happiness and peace, while
an aloe plant represented a good turn of luck. Similarly, finding
a four-leaf clover or the first flower of spring indicates your
fortunes are bound to improve.

One marvelous example of simple omen and sign reading that developed into a well-known, hands-on divination system comes from China. Here, the stalk of the yarrow plant was revered for its longevity. Then someone got the idea of cutting the stalks and using them in a rather intricate system that created hexagrams for the diviner to read. In 136 BC, this system was known as the Changes of Chow, which we now call the I-Ching. And, although the yarrow sticks are rarely used today for creating the hexes (coins have replaced the sticks), the system remains fairly unchanged and extremely popular... and it all began with a plant!

Another example originated in Greece where flowers were soaked with, or floated on, water and then observed. The Welsh have a different version of this system that uses a holly leaf and a candle. If the candle can float on the leaf in water, it symbolizes prosperity coming. Alongside these illustrations, there are even more types of *botanomancy* (divination with plants). The art of *daphnomancy* portends the future by the sound of burning laurel leaves, *Phyllorhodomancy* heeds the sound of rose leaves clapped together for omens, and *sycomancy* looks to the patterns of dried figs for insights. And that's just the beginning!

The modern practitioner has loads of tradition upon which to build their natural divination system. The purpose of this material is to provide you with some ideas on how to accomplish that in various practical and creative ways, some of which also have a history. While there is certainly nothing wrong with creating a wholly unique divination system that's born from your vision, using a historically verified method does have one advantage: the strong positive energies that grow out of hundreds, or even thousands of years of trust in that system. It also allows us to keep time-honored mystical arts from disappearing or remaining forever tucked away on a library shelf.

Random Omens and Signs

We've already talked briefly about how our ancestors observed nature for omens and signs to divine the future. Updating this idea a little bit for today's world isn't that difficult. Nature exists all around us, even for the urban dweller. We can view nature in window boxes, backyard gardens, nearby parks, on TV, in magazine pictures and fabric patterns, and frequently in the art with which we decorate our homes.

First, looking to flowers and plants that are living, we can begin by observing those that are around us regularly. Many people believe that the vibrations of an area affect flower and plant growth rates and vitality. So, if you've been focusing on a question, check to see what your houseplants are telling you! A sickly plant might indicate a similarly sickly relationship or situation that's not healthy for you, whereas two flowers intertwining might indicate emotional closeness.

Alternatively, if an unusual plant suddenly springs up in your yard, a window box, or a plant pot that you didn't sow, it could also represent a natural omen for you to ponder. For example, when I moved into a rented home, a wild rose began to grow along the fence. To me, this was a very positive sign for my marriage, and I considered it a lovely gift from the fairy folk.

The hard part of interpreting natural omens and signs is determining the difference between a happenstance and a real portent that comes from Earth's citizens, or the Divine speaking through nature's symbolism. I think the keys to recognizing the difference are uniqueness and frequency. As with my story above, it's not common to find a rosebush suddenly springing up on a city lawn. Or, if I started seeing roses growing everywhere I visited—on desks at the office, at stores, and so on (and it wasn't anywhere near Valentine's Day), the frequency of occurrence would be a cue to pay attention.

Now, observing a live plant for natural omens is one thing, but how do *we observe* man-made items? Actually, our two examples work with this, too. If you see the image of a plant or flower somewhere that you don't normally expect, that could be a sign for you to pay attention. For example, maybe someone paints a large graffiti tulip on an alleyway wall. This isn't the kind of thing you normally associate with graffiti! So, using the Correspondence List to guide the interpretive value, the appearance of this flower might mean your money troubles will soon be gone.

In terms of frequency, again keep your eyes open. If the same plant or flower shows up on advertisements, billboards, business cards, pamphlets, and the like, the constant repetition indicates something that calls for your attention. If a dandelion keeps appearing, it may reveal a knack for psychic impressions starting to blossom in your life. In the Language of Flowers, dandelions represent oracles.

Ultimately, you alone can decide what constitutes a real portent and what situations are just a coincidence. This means you have to keep your spiritual sensitivity keen. You don't want to go around trying to interpret every odd blade of grass. Remember: omens and signs come to us when we need them, acting as a gentle reminder that the spirits and the Divine can touch the here and now. More frequently, however, a flower is just a pretty flower, and that wilted geranium just needs water, not an over-spiritualized explanation!

Practical Considerations for Making an Oracle

In deciding among the various types of oracles I've presented in this material, you need to consider specific things.

First, how durable do you need your system to be? Someone with children or who travels regularly will want something that's not going to be easily damaged and is portable, so I'd suggest a stone or wood rune set.

Second, what flower and plant symbolism do you want to integrate, and how many items will the divination system have in total? I suggest settling on a minimum of thirteen plants that have enough variety of meanings to represent different, common human experiences (love, money, health, home, family, etc.). How you choose them is purely personal. You can, for example, use the Correspondence List at the end of this material to determine interpretive values. Or, you can create a wholly personal system based on your vision and the significance specific plants hold for you. The latter, or a combination of these two, is probably your best choice because you'll react positively to the finished product and be able to interpret it with ease.

Third, do you want your divination system to have a theme? For example, I made a Victorian flower set that featured lacy borders on the cards and popular blossoms from that era like rose, heather, and periwinkle. For each card's interpretive value, I turned to books on the Victorian language of flowers. This way the entire set resonated with a historic tone and flavor all its own. It also maintained a congruity of energy (it didn't mix symbolism or time periods).

Overall, I found the thematic approach worked very well for me and it might for you too. You could, for example, do a whole set on trees, bushes, or even roots! What's most important here is that you enjoy the theme you've chosen and that you write down the interpretive value of each symbol so you can continue to refer to it until you have them memorized.

The fourth consideration is simply how much time you have to devote to this. If you're very busy, you may wish to photocopy line drawings of plants or flowers, color them, and simply glue them to a sturdy surface. People with more time can get as elaborate as they wish (like making the pressed flower sets). Remember that our ancestors were very pragmatic, and time was often short for them too. It's more important that you have a system that's meaningful and works effectively for you than it is to have something entirely made by hand.

Casting Herbs or Flowers for Fortune-telling

This is one of the simpler methods of divination. It begins with either a napkin-size cloth or a large container of water (like a portable wash basin or a big mixing bowl). You will also need some flower petals, leaves, or other lightweight plant parts that represent the question at hand. Heather often corresponds with matters of beauty or luck, so if you were wondering whether someone finds you attractive or if your present fortune is going to change, this might be a good choice.

Next, take the cloth or water out beneath a full moon (this accents the intuitive nature). If you can't wait that long, the waxing moon is also suited to divination, as is working at night in front of a candle. I really don't recommend trying divination by day; sunlight encourages logic and the conscious mind, not psychism. If you have to try it during the day, go to a dimly lit room where you won't be disturbed and take a lit candle with you for a nice, mystical ambiance.

Toss your chosen petals and plant parts onto the surface of the water or cloth while thinking of a question. If you're using a cloth, look to see what patterns emerge (think of this as interpreting an inkblot). Or, you can decide ahead of time what various positions on the cloth represent and interpret the petals' meanings by where they land. For example, if all the petals land in the Western quarter of the cloth, this might indicate that there's a lot of emotion in your life right now (West is associated with feelings). Then if the rose petal lands in the Western quarter, I'd say love was on its way or that your life is presently filled with loving people!

NOTE: If you use placements for interpreting your casting, you can have different types of plant matter to broaden the diversity of readings, like having a rose petal (love), a daisy (youthful outlooks), a sunflower (the conscious mind), and so on.

If you're using water, you can watch for patterns as the petals float (like a fire spreading), or you can just pay attention to the direction in which the plant matter moves. Clockwise is positive as is an upward movement, or floating to the right. Counterclockwise, down, or left tends to be negative or indicates decreasing positive energy with regard to your question. If you drop the petals and they blow away before reaching the surface, that means that the situation is too complex to get a clear answer right now, or that something is changing very rapidly (the wind element emphasizes movement and transition).

When you're finished with the reading, you may wish to save the plant parts and make them into a charm for personal insight, or perhaps add them to a special divinatory incense that can be burned before a reading to clear the air and heighten your senses.

Flower/Herb Pendulums

Here's another marvelously easy method that anyone with a steady hand can try. For your pendulum divination to be as successful as possible, follow this seven-step guideline:

1. Pick a plant that represents the question at hand, and preferably one that's easily tied onto a string. Make sure it's free of debris (like bits of dirt) that can change the weight of your pendulum and skew the results of the effort.

2. Pick a colored string that also represents your goal. If you're not sure about color associations, here are the basics: red represents matters of love, energy, and power; yellow is the Air element for communication and creativity; green symbolizes growth, health, and money; blue is peace, joy, and the Water element; and purple represents matters of spirituality or leadership.

3. Cut the string so that it's slightly longer than the distance of your middle finger to your elbow.

4. Tie the chosen plant to one end so that it has a point (like a small group of flower petals with the tip pointing downward, or a root with the tip pointing downward).

5. Put the elbow of your stronger hand on a table and hold the other end of the string between your thumb and forefinger.

6. Steady the plant so it's still. Close your eyes and think about your question. Envision the details of your question as clearly as possible. When you feel the string moving, open your eyes.

7. Look at the pattern or direction of the plant's movements and make a mental note of it. Interpret this according to the list below.

You may want to repeat the entire exercise just to confirm the results. This is a good way to make sure your hand or elbow didn't accidentally move, or get moved by an outside source (like a pet rubbing up against you). Then, use this list as a general guideline for interpreting the plant pendulum's movements:

BOBBING: Uncertainty or hesitation; you may want to wait before acting. Alternatively, a difficult choice that really has two equal options.

CIRCLES: Peace, happiness, positive energy, good mental outlook about the situation at hand. Alternatively, the need to rely on the powerful aspects of self (leadership, courage, conscious mind).

DIAGONAL MOVEMENT: Conflict, something to overcome, possible physical problems that need attention.

ELLIPSES: Communication issues (North-South). East-West ellipses mean improvements in relationships as long as sensitivity is maintained. A diagonal ellipse speaks of ill motivation or an inability to assert yourself.

OVALS: The need to listen to the empathetic part of the self (the nurturing, inspired, sensitive aspects).

LEFT-RIGHT MOVEMENT: A level playing field. Alternatively, an overemphasis on the physical or a negative answer.

SQUARE-LIKE MOVEMENTS: Put foundations down before you reach for this goal. Alternatively, financial improvements.

UP-DOWN: Some type of division. Alternatively, a "yes" answer (like nodding one's head).

Decoupage on Stone, Wood, or Paper

This is a lovely way to make plant oracles for those who, like me, cannot draw anything but stick figures. To begin, you'll need either sturdy art paper (recycled if possible); a deck of blank cards (which can often be purchased at New Age or Occult gift shops); flat stones, crystals, or wood slices as the base media. You will also need a good-quality art spray or varnish and clipped images of the plants or flowers you want to use in your set.

I recommend looking for visually pleasing plant and flower images that either provide a symmetrical overhead view, or a full view leaf and all). My personal preference is plant pictures that have a definite upright position. The medieval wood engravings of flowers, for example, often show them with blossoms and roots (the blossom at the top indicating your upright positioning). Using these designs can cut your preparation time in half, allowing you to have *two* different meanings for the same card, stone, or wood slice (the upright, and the reversed). For example, if you choose tansy as one of your flowers, the upright position warns of conflict or an outright battle over something near to your heart. Reverse it, and it could mean the end of conflict and some sort of truce (literally turning over the leaf in energy and meaning, to use a familiar saying).

If the base media you've chosen is not pre-shaped, then you'll need to do that first. That way, you maintain symmetry in the finished product (in other words, cut out equal-size cards). If you're using stones or crystals, make sure to pick ones that are very close in size and shape and ones that also have a flat surface on which to glue your plant images. It doesn't matter if you use one kind of stone or several different types, as long as they're close in size and shape. However, when using a variety of stones, it's best to match the metaphysical correspondences of each crystal with that of the image it will bear (like using a tumbled amethyst with a white flower to represent peace).

If you're using wood, cut it so that each piece has the same diameter and thickness. One easy way to do this is to find a branch of the right thickness and slice equal segments off of it, followed by a good sanding so you don't get slivers when you handle them for readings. Or, cut a different type of wood for each symbol so that the base media and the flower or plant image match each other's energies. If you're handy with wood burning, you could burn plant images into the wood, literally ingraining the pattern of power on the surface. No matter how you make these, be sure to thank the Earth for its gift to you when you gather the wood.

Next, take the images you've gathered of the plants (be it cut out of a magazine, a photograph, or fabric) and put them on the base's surface. Move the image around a bit until you find the best placement—the one that feels right to you. It helps to keep the interpretive value of the plant or flower in mind when trying to do this. Then, using a pencil, trace the image onto your chosen surface. Glue the image on that spot.

After the glue has dried, you may want to add some type of press—apply lettering that labels the picture (this is entirely optional). You can also add a couple of drops of essential oil to each image so that the visual impact is coupled with aroma-therapy for impressive sensual cues.

Finish the media with art spray, varnish, or lacquer. This not only keeps the image in place, but protects the pieces from excess dirt. The choice of glossy or flat finish is purely personal, but I find that a flat finish tends to show off the images better. These need to dry completely. You may want to apply more than one protective coating for added sturdiness.

When the images are done, look over the set. Does it feel finished? Is something missing? Are any of the images off somehow? If so, now's the time to fine-tune the oracle. Fix whatever you feel needs fixing so that all the symbols work together harmoniously in your readings.

Last, but not least, take the time to review each card, stone, or wood slice separately. Now that it's finished, do you feel the completed work has a different meaning than what you originally intended, or what was given in this material? The creative process tends to have a special kind of magic all its own that often results in personalized variations. If this happens with your oracle, you need to make notes of interpretive variances somewhere so you can refer to them later.

Pressed Flower Oracle

This is a more difficult system to create and will take some time to develop. In this instance, you will actually be gathering fresh plant parts and pressing them for your oracle. There are several advantages to this approach to offset the effort involved, the first being the fact that you can time the plant's gathering to an auspicious moon or astrological phase so that it augments the symbol's energy. For example, if you were using the moonflower to represent the moon in your oracle, you might gather it by the light of the full moon so it's saturated with lunar vibrations.

The second advantage is having nature's voice speak to you more directly. Artistic renditions are fine, but there's nothing quite like the real thing for visual and spiritual impact. The plants already bear the energy signature of their correspondences (it's not something you have to try and achieve in your design), so it's quite likely that a pressed flower set will provide more accurate readings.

To begin with, you will have to make or buy a drying system. This tool allows you to dry and press a good amount of plant matter in about three weeks.

You can easily purchase one, but if you're the do-it-yourself type, you can make a functional drying press at home; it's not that hard. Begin with a flat board with 4–6 pieces of plain white paper (enough to cover the size of the board) on top. On the paper lay your ferns, flowers, and other plant pieces, leaving space in between so that they do not touch each other. Make sure they are not damp from the dew and are completely free of dirt. Put another 4–6 sheets of paper on top of this layer. Continue this way until you have a stack about 4–6 inches thick. Now, put another board on top of the bundle.

Next, you'll need two sturdy leather belts. Wrap the belts around the top and the bottom of this pile and pull them as tight as possible. Once a week, change the blotting paper and retighten the belts. If any of the plants adhere to the paper, just tap the back of the paper and they should come loose. Continue until the plant matter is completely dry and relatively flat.

An alternative to this is to wax the flower instead. This works best with semi-flat items like leaves, single petals, and fronds. Pick your item and let it dry a little in the sun. Then put it between two pieces of waxed paper (wax side toward the plant) and iron on low heat. This usually leaves the plant close to its original color, with a covering of wax to preserve it. It's important, however, to take the plant part out of the wax paper before it cools or it will remain stuck between the layers. If that happens, just warm the sheets again with the iron and release your treasure.

Once you've completed these steps, you can go back to arranging, gluing, and varnishing for a lovely decoupage effect. An alternative to using varnish for your cards is to use a clear plastic laminate over each card (you can often have this done at photocopy stores). The only disadvantage here is that plastic tends to scratch after a while.

Blessing Your Oracle

After all that hard work, don't forget to bless and charge your oracle. Blessing invites your image of the Divine to touch and fill your divination tool so it will respond to you more intimately. Generally, a blessing is accomplished by holding your hands palm-down over the tool and reciting an invocation or prayer of your choosing. One blessing you can use is:

> *"Lord of the Sun, Lady Moon, see the work of my hands. I ask that you bless this tool to provide insight when my own vision is lacking, or when a friend needs aid. When in use, let the intuitive energies flow freely, balanced ever by conscious responsibility for my gifts and how I use them. Let all readings be shared for the greatest good, and may I ever hear your voice in my efforts. So be it."*

As with all magic, change the wording so it better suits the tool and your personal path. You need not get fancy here. The God/dess cares more about intention than elaborate words.

When you're done, leave the oracle, in whatever form you made it, in sunlight for three hours and full moonlight for three hours. This charges the oracle with both conscious and psychic energies so your readings will be balanced. When you notice your oracle begin to give you information that's "off," bless it again (this helps eliminate unwanted energies), and recharge it.

Potential Layouts for Your Oracle

Your finished oracle can be used in conjunction with almost any of the traditional tarot or rune layouts that are found in any number of books. The only restriction here is that the layout's positions cannot exceed the total number of symbols you have created for your oracle. Be that as it may, since this system is highly personalized and in touch with your vision, it might be worthwhile to consider creating your own layout designs.

To these ends, and in an effort to offer you greater flexibility and a working model, you can consider the layouts that follow here as one option. Since the deck I created was based on the Victorian Language of Flowers, I made layouts that, to me, represented nature's voice and specifically the flowers in a variety of ways, combined with two other layouts that were common in every tarot and rune book I've ever seen. Many of these layouts are very adaptable to other thematic sets, so I think you'll find them helpful in making your own.

You will notice that most layouts include a significator. This represents the person asking the question. You can choose this symbol at random or find one that best represents that individual in its upright position. The layouts also include a sample reading based on the correspondences list accompanying this material. That way, you have an example to refer to in trying each layout to see which, if any, you'd like to use for your own oracle.

THE DAILY GUIDANCE LAYOUT

This is pretty straightforward. Just go to your oracle and randomly pick out one symbol. Read the interpretive value you've assigned to that symbol to prepare yourself for whatever lies ahead that day. For example, if you were going on a job interview and pulled an inverted honeysuckle image, that would indicate the need for caution. Honeysuckle reversed means something's being misrepresented to you. So if it appears too good to be true, it probably is!

PAST, PRESENT, AND FUTURE LAYOUT

This is a very simple and quick layout to use when you want a little more perspective regarding a fairly uncomplicated matter. The significator is placed at **A** (for this layout, the significator card is chosen randomly), the past is indicated by **B**, the present by **C**, and the future or outcome by **D**.

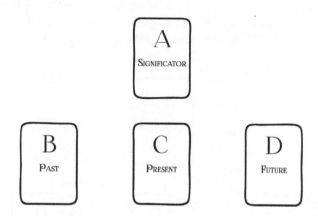

Let's say you were considering a move, and wondered how (or if) it would affect your relationships. The result was **A** jasmine reversed, **B** zinnia upright, **C** buttercup upright, and **D** carnation upright. This might be interpreted as saying that you need to be sensible. Look closely at the situation from various angles before making any decision. In the past, there's been some type of ending or separation that's left you worrying about present relationships. Do not allow what was to influence what is.

If you see there's some type of financial improvement on the horizon, and if you were considering moving to get a new job, this would be a good omen. Even so, nothing is coming in the immediate future, so be patient. Finally, the outcome card is one of success and reason for celebration, including professional recognition. Overall, I'd say the move would be a good thing.

FOUR WINDS LAYOUT

This is where the layout designs really begin to reflect the natural world. The significator **A** (again chosen at random for this spread) is placed in the middle of the winds; **B** represents the East wind, which speaks of business, intellect, and things about which we hope; **C** represents the South wind, filled with energy, power, and dramatic changes; **D** is the Westerly wind that's emotional and fertile; and finally, **E** is the North wind that councils us on matters of health, foundations, and the need for patience.

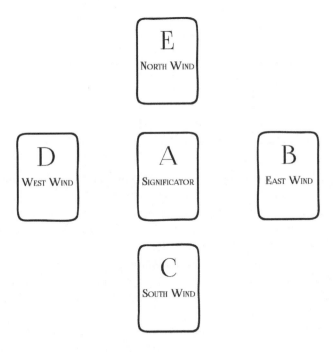

Putting this into an actual question, say you were asking why certain cycles keep repeating in your life. The reading layout shows **A** as the evergreen upright, **B** as iris reversed, **C**

as clover upright, **D** as balm upright, and **E** as holly reversed. I would interpret this as saying you lack self-confidence to the point where you make others ill at ease. Until this changes, relationships with people may always be a bit rocky. In the East, we see how you are always taking on too much as if to impress others. Unless you slow down and do one thing well, it may be hard to gain the respect you so desperately desire.

In the South, the upside of the equation says you have some really good ideas. You can see potential in situations and could be very successful once you learn to really focus. The West follows up on this advice by saying you need to overcome the need for external approval. The real motivating force for personal improvements must come from within or the cycle will continue to repeat itself.

Finally, to the North, this card advises this individual to think long and hard before jumping into a conversation. Yes, you have good ideas, but your insecurity makes you come off like a know-it-all, even when you obviously don't! When you learn the value of both silence and speech and when to use both, it will help break the cycle of negative relationships and build your self-confidence.

The Five Petal Layout (a Pentagram)

This layout is designed to help you attune to specific spiritual interests since the petals here are laid out like a pentagram. **A** is the significator (chosen at random); **B** represents psychic influences in your life, the apex of the question, or the things that require careful consideration; **C** speaks of your physical self or monetary matters; **D** symbolizes purifying energy—the things that need a little bit of heat to inspire growth and change; **E** reveals hidden matters—the things that lie just beneath the surface of a situation; finally **F** is the outcome—what will happen if the progression continues as it stands in the layout. See illustration on the next page.

For this layout, let's consider a question about whether or not to join a specific study group. In response, the reading shows **A** as almond upright, **B** as daisy upright, **C** as buttercup reversed, **D** as fennel upright, **E** as myrtle upright, and **F** as carnation upright. Beginning with the almond, this indicates a good reason to hope as long as you don't let that enthusiasm get out of control. This combined with **B**, which indicates you have very good intentions, opens the reading on a positive note.

C says that you shouldn't just accept your first impressions of any group you're considering. If any of them asks for money in particular, I'd say the warning bells should go off. **D** indicates that a little of your past is influencing the way you're handling the present search, specifically a fear of interacting with others. **E** says you will find the right group eventually, as long as you don't give up when you think you're not making any progress, and **F** confirms this with a symbol of joy and success.

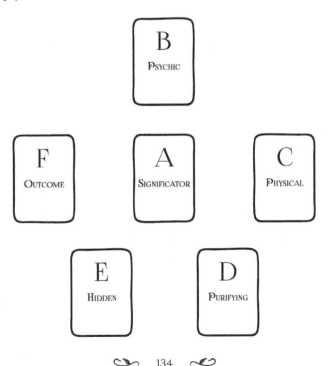

SIX PETAL LAYOUT (HEXAGRAM)

In this layout, the significator (either chosen randomly or purposefully) **A** is, once again, placed in the middle; **B** represents an overview of the situation and any significant influences on same; **C** represents matters of the recent past that are still being felt; **D** indicates present emotions, actions, or thoughts with regard to the question; **E** is the card of hidden matters or what you're not seeing directly or immediately; **F** represents the actions called for now or in the very near future; and **G** is your outcome card.

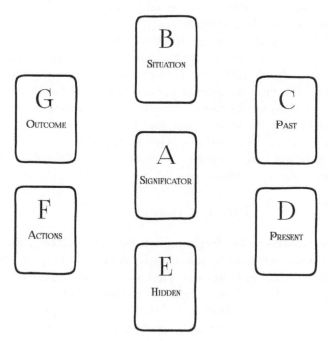

For the purpose of this layout, we'll use the question: Should I accept the position I was just offered? The results of the layout were: **A** as dandelion upright, **B** as honeysuckle upright, **C** as lilac reversed, **D** as fennel upright, **E** as clover reversed, **F** as moss reversed, and **G** as myrtle upright. Starting with **A**, the significator indicates a serious case of butterflies on your part. For some reason, there's a sense of discomfort about either the job or the company.

The overview, **B**, indicates that you need to trust yourself to do the right thing. In my divination system, the honeysuckle indicates honest dealings and personal integrity. So, no matter what others say, listen to your heart.

In the recent past, **C**, there was some type of interest that consumed you to the point of distraction. Your actions during this period directly affect the present, **D**, which is a card of both protection and strength. To me, this symbolizes an overall concern as to whether you're fully equipped to handle the position that's been offered.

The foundation of the whole situation, **E**, speaks of bad luck, frustration, and awkward circumstances. Whatever led up to this job offer, it's been a rough ride that's left you out of focus. This directly relates to **F**, the action called for. Take your time and get some perspective before doing anything. Don't get caught up in the moment and don't be capricious.

Finally, the outcome card, **G**, says that whatever your decision is, you should stand by it tenaciously. Your devotion and conviction will motivate you, not other people's opinions.

THE FULL FLOWER LAYOUT

This layout is perfect for getting detailed answers. Here, position **S** is your significator (either chosen randomly or purposefully). This position indicates the questioner's prevalent mood and thoughts. **A** is the base of the flower and the root of the situation. This is the most difficult part of this layout to interpret because it's figuratively underground, denoting hidden matters.

B indicates circumstances or people that promote the difficulty or situation at hand; **C** is the card of obstacles, that which impedes progress or causes general frustration; **D** speaks of things in the recent past that may have direct bearing on the situation; **E** is the immediate future if things continue along the same path; **F** is the here and now, the present and most personally

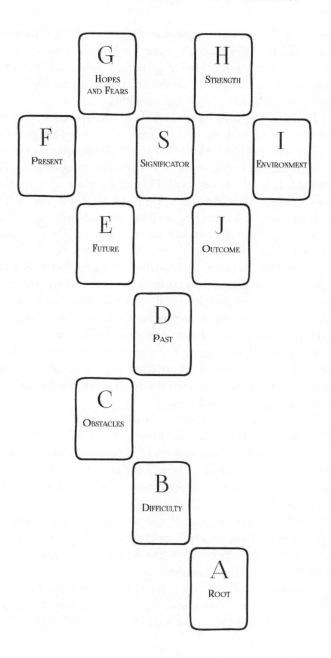

significant factors in this question; **G** is the card that indicates hopes and fears; **H** portends something or someone in which you will find strength or encouragement; **I** is the environment in which you're working, and advises as to personal actions in that environment; and finally **J** is the outcome.

To illustrate this layout, let's use the question: What's the best course of action for success in applying my personal talents? When I used my Flower cards for this question posed by a friend, the results were **A** as lavender upright, **B** as lilac reversed, **C** as clover reversed, **D** as chamomile upright, **E** as moss upright, **F** as almond upright, **G** as aspen reversed, **H** as daisy upright, **I** as myrtle upright, and **J** as holly upright.

The significator card was chosen specifically so that it represented my friend, so I won't interpret it here.

At the base, **A**, of the question, we had a card that indicated a very positive decision. The answer to her heart's desire was right around the corner. Building on this root, we have a warning for her not to completely immerse herself in this new course of action. Be consistent and even-tempered for best results.

Obstacles, **C**, were going to come, mostly in the form of bad luck. Minor annoyances, unexpected expenditures, and other small difficulties may dampen the spirit a bit. Even so, it's not worth getting all worked up about.

In the recent past, my friend had been working very hard to guide herself toward a specific goal. Considering the rest of the cards, this was time well spent. The immediate future, **E**, indicated a new friend or beneficial acquaintance appearing in her life—possibly a teacher who could help her further hone her skills.

Moving to the present, **F**, she seemed to have an anxious but upbeat outlook, which is perfectly normal. She shouldn't let her nerves get the best of her. The winds were turning to blow at her back, so patience was the key.

Position **G** said that her greatest fear was steeped in a lack of self-confidence. Old insecurities were nagging at her, and they needed to be left in the past where they belonged. While the importance of this question seemed overwhelming then, the insecurity was just a by-product of her hope for success.

The greatest strength she has to help her presently, **H**, was a pure, childlike joy in life and very good intuitive senses. She had to use her joy to meet difficulties, and trust that inner voice more!

The call for action in this situation was **I**, to remain enthusiastic. She should stick with her idea and not let naysayers get the best of her. If she could do this, the outcome card, **J**, revealed she would have good cause for celebration. She just had to maintain her focus, keep organized, and be ready for opportunity to knock.

Ultimately, the cards showed that almost anything goes and it will all go her way!

With all these layouts, I've used my own set of flower cards and illustrative questions so you can see a little bit of how one symbol builds on the others in a reading. Also, my interpretations and yours could be totally different if you've ascribed personal meanings to your oracle, let alone chosen completely different flowers and plants! This is really the wonderful part about using nature for divination. Her gifts are plentiful, meaning each person's oracle can be as unique as they are.

The Art of the Diviner

When you go to use your oracle, please do so with a gentle voice. Such a lovely tool is not meant for gloom and doom, and it also should not be used to push your personal opinion on others through a third party. A good diviner knows when they cannot put personal feelings aside for a reading, or when they're too tired or out-of-sorts to read effectively. You will need to develop this kind of honesty with yourself and others if you plan on reading with any type of regularity.

Additionally, a good diviner knows that tools are just that: tools. They are not the end-all and be-all of our spirituality. We should not use divination systems, even those from nature, as a crutch or guru. That's not the purpose for which they're made. Instead, let them be a guide and helpmate when perspective is dimmed.

In working with readers around the country, almost all of them offer some basic advice, which I've assembled here for you. Look it over. I think you'll find it very helpful no matter what divination system you undertake:

- If you're reading for yourself, only do so if you can maintain an unbiased outlook when you're interpreting the symbols. If you're too emotional or too involved, get help from another reader.
- If you're sick, tired, stressed out, or otherwise out of sorts, don't try to do a reading for yourself or anyone else. The results are bound to be negative just because your physical or emotional state isn't at its peak.
- Consider creating a pre-reading mini-ritual for yourself that helps put you in the right frame of mind for psychic work. Some people pray, others meditate, others still light candles, play an instrument, or burn incense. A lot depends on what actions heighten the reader's awareness. Once you find a system that works for you, use it regularly. This way it becomes a spiritual cue, signaling the higher self about what's ahead.
- Keep a journal for personal layouts. This serves two purposes. First, you can refer back to it anytime to reconsider the reading in light of what has since transpired. Second, as you see your oracle working successfully in these pages, it will build confidence. This confidence improves the overall accuracy of future readings and helps in further honing the oracle.
- Always advise the people for whom you read that they are responsible for their fate. The oracle does not create the future, it only reads the most likely one at that moment.

- Always try to present bad news in a proactive, positive way. No one should leave a reading frightened or feeling helpless.
- As time goes on, regularly review your oracle to see if you need to adapt it, add to it, or create something wholly new. As you grow and change as a person, your divination tools often need to be transformed to reflect those transitions. Your fortune-telling set might suddenly seem way too simple, or just feel as if it doesn't fit anymore, like shoes that are too small. If you've found that your tools don't reflect you anymore, you can give them away. The new owner can cleanse them and attune them to their personal energy and vibrations. These two possibilities are a strong indication that it's time to find a fresh divinatory tool that appeals to your spiritual maturity and higher senses.
- Always stay open to the voice of Spirit, no matter what symbols come up in a reading. Sometimes a person needs to hear something about a different subject. If you're open to Spirit, you can help meet that need.
- Last, but not least, always take time to cleanse your oracle and yourself after a reading. Shake off any energy that accumulates on your hands and arms so that you don't accidentally pick up negative residue. Put your divinatory tool away in a special place where it won't get handled a lot, and one that keeps it clean and safe from damage. People often ask whether personal tools can be handled by others without affecting the tool's energy. I believe that the touch/don't touch "rule" is really a matter of preference.

In my years of using all kinds of divination systems, I have found these guidelines to be sound. Since you've made your fortune-telling tool yourself, it should already be responding to you very positively. These suggestions and hints fill out the rest of the divination equation by making sure the tools respond positively to a wide variety of reading settings and situations.

Prefabricated Systems

Some people have very busy schedules that don't really allow for making an oracle from scratch. For those readers, I'd suggest going to New Age gift shops and seeing what's on the market. In particular, the following tarot decks have natural themes: *The Herbal Tarot* by Michael Tierra, the *Celtic Tree Oracle* by Colin Murray, the *Crop Circle Cards* by Cariel Quinly, the *Greenwood Tarot* by Mark Ryan, and the *Healing Flower Color Cards* by Ingrid Kraaz.

Once you find a ready-made system that appeals to both your inner and outer visions, remember to bless it and find suitable housing for it, just as I described for hand-made oracles. Just because you couldn't make it yourself doesn't mean the divination system will be any less accurate or less meaningful. Treat your magical tools like good friends, and they will always respond in kind.

Chapter 7

Spicy Spells and Charms

> *"All nature is a vast symbolism; every material fact*
> *has sheathed within it a spiritual truth."*
> —Edwin H. Chapin

You might see the above quote, or something similar, posted prominently in a Green Witch's home. It speaks volumes about where we find our magic, and how precious that discovery process is to our questing spirit. After taking the time to get to know Earth's voice, its symbols, and energies—after growing some of our own flowers and herbs, cooking and brewing with them, or decorating our homes with them—we will most certainly want to weave spells and create charms with these gifts from Gaia. It's just another (if you'll excuse the pun) "natural" outgrowth of being a Green Witch.

In writing this material, I faced an organizational dilemma, however. Would you want your spells and charms topically arranged, or prefer them by plant type? Since this material is about flora and its applications, I chose the latter and put the greenery in alphabetical order for ease of reference. However, each spell and charm have a theme in boldface at the outset to make things easier for those readers who would have preferred the alternative.

The next problem I faced was what to include or exclude! There's a lot to choose from in nature's domain. Here again, I had to rely on personal preference—the flowers, spices, and other plant parts that I use most often in my green magic. Don't let this sampling hinder your creativity. Hopefully, the Correspondence List will fill in any gaps that this material cannot.

ALFALFA

Old wives' tales say that any home that has alfalfa growing will always know providence.

MONEY CHARM: So long as you have a healthy alfalfa plant growing in your home, you will never want. (This doesn't mean being wealthy, it simply means having your needs met.)

QUICK MONEY SPELL: Snip pieces from your alfalfa plant when the moon is full. Dry these and burn just a few whenever you need cash quickly.

APPLE

Green Witches love apples, not simply to keep the doctor away but because they offer so many potential components, each with a slightly different symbolic value—seeds, rind, wood, and flowers.

YOUTH CHARM: If it was good enough for the Norse gods, it's good enough for us. According to this tradition, simply eating apples regularly not only improves health but restores youthful energy.

LAND BLESSING SPELL: Take a wand fashioned from apple wood and walk the land with it, moving clockwise, as you say *"Mother Earth, grow lush and green. Let all that dwells in this soil be fertile and yield abundantly.*" Repeat the incantation until you've covered the area in one complete circuit.

BALM

Paracelsus (a sixteenth-century Swiss alchemist) called this herb "the elixir of life." It has retained that honor in modern society in that we call a healing salve a "balm."

ANXIETY CHARM: Gather some lemon balm and put it in a cotton drawstring bag or a tea ball. Empower this by saying "When taken within, let peace begin. Anxiety cease, as the magic's released." Carry this with you and steep it in hot water for a calming tea when needed.

JOY SPELL: Take a fresh balm leaf and rub it over your heart chakra saying *"Joy, joy, joy within, by my will the magic begins. Sadness depart, restore joy to my heart."* Dry the leaf on your altar, and when the spell manifests, burn it with a prayer of thankfulness.

BASIL

One of the folk names for basil is "Witch's herb." In India, it's a traditional funerary herb, especially for prominent leaders.

AFFECTION CHARM: Plant a pot of basil and tend to it lovingly. When it's growing heartily, give it to someone you love. This encourages love and devotion.

BANISHING SPELL: Put a symbol or word on a fresh basil leaf that represents what you want to banish. Leave this in the light of the sun to dry. When dried, pound the leaf into minute parts and burn it. This will release the negative energy.

Bay

Bay was often part of the incense used at the Delphic oracle to improve divinatory abilities. It is sacred to Apollo.

Energy Charm: Bind bay together with marigold petals in a yellow, orange, or gold color sachet and carry it with you for increased vitality. This also provides a strong protective energy.

Romance Spell: Take a fresh bay leaf and rub it into the surface of a pink candle (or one of a color that symbolizes romance to you). Twirl the candle clockwise in one hand, holding the leaf on its surface with the other, saying thrice "Me and you and we; let love have its way and romance dance free!" Light the candle when you're spending time with your significant other.

Blackberry

Blackberry pie is among the traditional Pagan foods for Lammas because its abundant nature typifies the first harvest.

Protection Charm: Take a small, dead blackberry branch with the brambles and soak it in water overnight. Once it's pliable, bend it into a circle and place it around an item that symbolizes that which needs safety and protection. Leave the brambles and the item in place until the trouble passes. At this point, you can grind the wood into powder and use it as a base in a warding incense.

Wealth Spell: Wrap a large blackberry leaf around a silver coin (real silver would be best). Take a braid of gold, silver, and green thread to bind this in place saying, *"Where gold and green are joined, blessed herewith by a silver coin, wealth and prosperity, to me…to me."*

BUTTERCUP

Irish farmers trusted in buttercups to improve the yield of butter from cream or milk from cows to produce that cream.

MONEY CHARM: Carry a dried, pressed, or waxed buttercup in your pocket to promote prosperity. To increase the effectiveness, bind the buttercup together with a silver coin inside a green cloth during a waxing to full moon or better yet, on May Day.

HEALTH SPELL: Take the petals of a dried buttercup and remove them from the plant saying, *"Heal my body, make me well, heed the words within my spell."* Toss the petals on a fire and let them burn completely, then sprinkle the ashes with salt. This is an adaptation of a medieval healing charm especially suited to mental illness.

CARNATION

In Korea, carnations are used for fortune-telling. During the Middle Ages, they were added to curatives to combat fever.

COURAGE CHARM: Simply pinning this flower to your scarf or lapel is said to inspire courage and bravery. It is also a sign of honor. To add more magic to the equation, bless the carnation, saying *"Carnations of valor to have and to hold, by this magic make me bold!"*

ANTI-ANGER SPELL: Take a carnation in your hand. Focus your negative feelings and let them saturate the flower. Continue until you feel empty. Next, put the carnation in the freezer to quite literally "chill out!"

CHAMOMILE

A wise Green Witch grows this herb in their garden to make everything therein healthy, lush, and fertile.

MONEY CHARM: When you want to hold on to your cash, wash it before you go out, in a chamomile tincture. According to tradition, this either draws money or helps you save it.

SOLAR SPELL: To saturate your aura with all the attributes of the Sun, bathe at noon on Midsummer's Day in chamomile-laden water. As you do, visualize your body being filled with the golden rays of the Sun, and any negativity washing away down the drain.

CHRYSANTHEMUM

The name of this blossom means *"golden flower."* It is the national flower of Japan, while in China, Buddhists believe that Keu Tze Tung's sacred stories were written on dewy chrysanthemum petals.

LONGEVITY CHARM: People of the Far East believe that these flower petals grant long life to a person, project, or relationship. So, keep some fresh or dried chrysanthemum petals near those things you hold dear and want to last. Don't forget to bless them, perhaps by saying *"Golden flower from the Sun, by my will, this spell's begun. See in me a heart pure, that this _____ may endure."* (Fill in the blank according to your goal.)

SMILE SPELL: Quickly blanch some chrysanthemum petals and toss them in a bowl with a hint of vinegar and some chopped egg, then eat. This internalizes improved disposition.

Cinnamon

The Hebrews and the Arabs were among the first civilizations to use cinnamon in perfumes. More importantly, in the Middle East, cinnamon is among the anointing oils suited for use in the temple.

Attention Charm: If you're having trouble focusing, bind a cinnamon stick together with a tourmaline stone and keep it in the room where you need conscious awareness the most.

Love Spell: Dip the pointer finger of your dominant hand in powdered cinnamon and trace a heart over your heart chakra saying, *"As this spell is spoken, as the magic unfolds, bring to me a love that's true—one to have and one to hold."* Sprinkle a little extra cinnamon outside your door so that love can follow you home.

Clove

Cloves were among the most expensive spices in the ancient world, often worth as much as cattle!

Serenity Charm: Folklore tells us that simply smelling this herb when you're tense or anxious will encourage an easygoing disposition.

Kinship Spell: To improve the sense of unity among a group, gather one whole clove for each person in that group and bless it. Disperse the cloves among the group and have everyone carry them in a wallet or purse regularly.

Clover

In Scotland, people sometimes created a milk bath with clover to alleviate melancholy. Druids felt it was a potent amulet against evil.

Love Charm: Put a four-leaf clover in your shoe and love will walk with you.

Luck Spell: Pick a full clover, leaves and all, and gently turn the leaves counterclockwise until they break off saying *"Bad luck turn, turn, turn away, burn, burn, burn away."* As you say the last part, burn the leaves. Carry the head of the flower with you for protection and improved fortune.

Corn

The spirit of corn was often said to guard the fields and provide fertility. A Green Witch would do well to use a few kernels in the soil to protect and nourish the land.

Providence Charm: Carry a few kernels of dried corn (or popcorn) in your pocket. When you need providence quickly, release one to the Earth and let that energy grow.

Blessing Spell: Sprinkled colored corn (use food coloring) around the perimeter of your sacred space while quietly chanting this verse adapted from a favorite magical song: *"Corn and grain, corn and grain, all that falls shall rise again. Around the circle, and where it goes, there shall our magic flow!"*

Daisy

Daisies are the traditional decoration for Midsummer festivals. According to lore, these flowers sprang from Mary Magdalene's tears.

SOLAR CHARM: Once the daisy was called "day's eye" because it turns its face to follow the sun. In keeping with this, pick a daisy at noon on a bright sunny day and carry it with you to augment solar energies (the conscious mind, strength, and leadership).

FIDELITY SPELL: Take a freshly picked daisy and slowly remove its petals saying, *"Love be true, love be kind, in these petals my magic bind."* Burn these petals just before meeting your lover, or carry them with you to the next rendezvous.

DANDELION

The patroness of Witches, Hecate, once entertained Theseus with dandelion wine. In the language of flowers, it represents ancient oracles.

ANTI-MAGIC CHARM: In Sicilian tradition, gathering a handful of dandelion heads on St. John's Eve (Midsummer) ensures the wearer of protection from Witches.

PSYCHISM SPELL: To improve your powers of spiritual insight, make a tea out of dandelion flowers and leaves. Stir it clockwise saying, *"Open my eyes and let me see beyond the veil, my spirit freed."* Drink the tea to internalize this flower's energy just before divination efforts.

DILL

Binding dill to a home was once a very common anti-magic charm. Perhaps this protective power is why the Greeks used dill as part of decorative crowns for heroes.

YIN-YANG CHARM: According to magical tradition, dill promotes a healthy balance between the conscious and unconscious mind, the esoteric and mundane. Smell it or carry it to help create this balance.

Luck Spell: Take a loaf of frozen bread dough and allow it to rise. Knead in a personally pleasing amount of dill, then bake according to the directions on the package. The heat and the rising of the bread will both activate and release fortunate energy.

Geranium

Rural lore in the United States claims that snakes will not cross the path of this plant. More practically, place it in your windows to keep flies away.

Hospitality Charm: To encourage the arrival of desired guests in your home, and make them feel welcome once they arrive, simply pick some fresh geraniums and bring them indoors. Put them in water and place them in your living room.

Fertility Spell: Pick a white geranium and carry it close to your heart (as you would keep a child emotionally close). When the flower dries, burn it, whispering your wishes into the smoke. You can also rub this flower on your threshold to bless all who dwell within your home.

Ginger

This was such a beloved herb to the ancients that people said it was first grown in Eden!

Health Charm: Find a piece of ginger root that resembles a person, then wrap a piece of fabric from an old piece of your clothing around it. As long as you keep this safe, it will promote well-being.

Consecration Spell: To dedicate your athame, burn some ginger on a fire source and move the blade through it as you invoke your vision of the Divine and ask for their blessings. Ginger not only helps with the consecration process but also increases the amount of magical energy with which you have to work.

Heather

Heather was often featured in the initiation rites of Scottish Witches. In this region, it was also believed that sleeping on a bed stuffed with heather will keep you healthy.

Rain Charm: Burn a little dried heather or heather-scented incense when you want to invoke rain.

Cleansing Spell: On Midsummer's Day, it's customary to use a sprig of heather to asperge the sacred space. Dip the heather in spring water and move clockwise around the circle saying, *"East and South, West and North, beauty and blessing now come forth!"*

Iris

These lovely flowers bear the name of the Greek goddess of the rainbow. Its three petals are said to represent bravery, discernment, and faith.

Faith Charm: When you need to trust in yourself more, or in a specific ideal, bathe in water that has iris petals floating in it. Afterward, dry one of the petals and carry it with you.

Goddess Spell: When you want to focus on the feminine aspect of the Divine, use this spell. Pick an iris and put it on your altar saying *"One petal is the Maiden, the next the Mother, the third the Crone. All are welcome in my sacred space of home!"* Refresh the flower as necessary.

Lavender

Roman sex workers used the aroma of lavender to attract clients. Wearing a sprig near your head during the fall helps keep colds at bay.

ANTI-ABUSE CHARM: If you suffer emotional abuse from those around you, tuck a piece of lavender in a bag and wear it near your heart. It will help banish the negative words, and give you greater inner strength.

DREAM SPELL: Gather a piece of fresh lavender just before going to bed on the night of waxing to the full moon. Hold the lavender in your hand and say, *"Flower of blue, bring dreams that come true!"* It is said that if you have a dream, it will soon come true.

LEMON

Among the Strega (Italian Witches), it was common to use a lemon as an alternative to poppets.

FRIENDSHIP CHARM: When you're hoping to make new friends, carry a few lemon seeds in your pocket, or some lemon-flavored candies. Scatter a seed or eat the candy just before going into a social situation.

SOUL-MATE SPELL: On the night of a full moon, peel off the rind of a lemon in one piece. Keep this in a safe place and it will draw your soulmate to you. Once you find them, burn a little of the rind any time you need to refresh the relationship.

LILAC

It's considered bad luck to wear lilacs on May Day. It means you will never marry. On the other hand, bathing in lilac water on May Day makes you more beautiful!

ANTI-GHOST CHARM: Simply planting lilacs near your home or office will keep the entire area safe from any unhappy, wandering souls.

HAPPY LOVE SPELL: For this spell, you need to gather a few white and purple lilacs (white is for joy, and purple is to inspire adoration). Take these to a windy location, if possible where the wind is blowing from the South (warmth), and release the petals saying *"Let there be joy in my love. Let this relationship be blessed by the God and Goddess above."*

MARIGOLD

The predominant myth about this plant is that it originally grew out of the blood of those slain during Cortes's conquest of Mexico.

ANTI-GOSSIP CHARM: Picking this flower in August and keeping it with a bay leaf turns all wagging tongues away.

ANTI-ANXIETY SPELL: Marigold is a flower of the Sun, so it's most potent when picked at noon. Take your noonday blossom in hand saying *"The light of the sun shines on my heart. Chase the shadows, all sadness depart!"* Tear up the flower and release it to the Earth to release your anxiety.

MARJORAM

This herb is sacred to Venus, so it's not surprising to discover that it is used for both love spells and love divinations.

DREAM LOVER CHARM: Put a bundle of marjoram under your pillow (fresh is best) and it will bring you dreams of a future love, or sweet dreams of someone you hold dear.

REST SPELL: When you've been feeling uneasy and need to calm your spirit, drink a cup of marjoram tea that's been stirred counterclockwise (banishing) while saying *"Anxiety cease, tension release!"*

Mint

Mint is one of the most versatile magical herbs because it comes in so many varieties including sage, lemon, peppermint, and pennyroyal.

Study Charm: Dab a little mint on the corners of your books and your temples to improve your concentration. Or, enjoy a mint tea and internalize its energies.

Sweet Words Spell: When you need your communications to be particularly gentle and sweet, use this spell. Begin with several fresh mint leaves steeped in warm water to make a tea. Stir this clockwise saying thrice: *"By this charm I now repeat, let my words be ever sweet!"* Rinse your mouth with the tea just before your conversation occurs.

Orchid

Greek legends tell us that Satyrs loved this flower as a snack, and they are edible!

Friendship Charm: Tradition tells us that simply wearing this flower promotes friendship. Or, you can present it to someone as a way of opening the door to improved relationships.

Passion Spell: This spell uses the root of the orchid rather than the flower. Begin by boiling a little sliced root (¼ inch is fine) in water. To this, add a little lemon juice and orange rind saying, *"Passion and zeal, bring me sex appeal!"* Eat to internalize the energy. An alternative is to bless some petals and have them on a sandwich.

PANSY

Also known as "kiss-me-quick," this flower also symbolizes thought. Folklore has it that the pansy once had an aroma, but prayed to have it removed so people wouldn't ruin fields just to acquire it.

RAIN CHARM: Pick a pansy at dawn, which represents hopefulness, and sprinkle water on it. Rain will follow.

LOVE SPELL: Again, you should pick your flower at dawn. Tie it gently onto a string about three feet long. Put this across from you at a table. Begin chanting *"Love, love, come to me"* as you slowly draw the flower toward your heart chakra. When the string is used up, carry the flower until your spell manifests.

PARSLEY

In the Victorian Language of Flowers, this represents socialization, whereas, during the Middle Ages, people consumed parsley to allay rowdiness and drunkenness.

CELEBRATION CHARM: If you're desirous of having an occasion for feasting and merriment, cut parsley from your garden on Good Friday. This also attracts more luck into your life.

CHEERFULNESS SPELL: Rub a fresh sprig of parsley on your forehead, temples, and heart chakra (in that order) saying *"Let my mind focus on happy thoughts, my ears hear only good news, and my heart overflow with joy."* Dry the sprig and use it for an uplifting incense later.

PERIWINKLE

I love this flower's charming name. People in England and France sometimes refer to this flower as the "Sorcerer's Violet" because of its use as a protective amulet.

ANTI-ENVY CHARM: Wash your hands in spring water, then pluck this flower on either the first, ninth, eleventh, or thirteenth night of the moon and carry it with you. This protects you from those who would do you harm and also grants abundance.

Peaceful Spirit Spell: If you feel that someone's spirit is not resting quietly, go and sprinkle periwinkle petals on their grave saying, *"May your wandering cease, let your spirit find peace."* In Welsh tradition, this is thought to help children's spirits especially.

PRIMROSE

If you'd like to use primroses in a clock garden, the evening primrose will close with a loud click come nightfall.

GARDEN CHARM: Simply plant primrose bushes at the four corners of your garden, or in a central location, to ensure the growth and lushness of everything therein.

FAIRY SPELL: To attract fairies or improve your rapport with them, place some fresh primroses on your altar saying *"Spirits of the fairy world, hear my wish, heed my words. Come dance with me in the sacred space, while working magic in this place!"* Be aware of any changes that happen after this, and have some little gifts (like sweet bread) ready to place on windows or doorways as an offering.

ROSE

Roses are sacred to a variety of gods and goddesses including Eros, Cupid, Demeter, and Isis. There are over ten thousand known varieties of this flower.

LOVE CHARM: Begin with equal portions of cinnamon, ginger, rosewater, powdered clove, nutmeg, myrrh, and dried rose petals. Blend these together and crush them until very well mixed. Add a few drops of pink wax and form this into a ball. Once dried, place this in any area where you want emotional warmth to fill the room.

UNITY SPELL: For this spell, you'll need to make a garland of roses long enough to go around two people's wrists (you may use silk roses dabbed with oil as an alternative to fresh ones, otherwise carefully remove the thorns). As you make the strand say *"Aphrodite, great goddess of love, bind your blessing in these your flowers till they wrap 'round the wrists of two who are promised to each other. There, release your power into their hearts that they may never part."*

You can now use this strand as part of a handfasting (bind the wrists with the garland at the end of the ritual to denote unity). You can also alter the incantation so it applies to other kinds of unity (such as business partnerships), and then use the strand in your alliance ritual.

ROSEMARY

Rosemary was favored in Hungarian beauty preparations. Romans trusted in this herb to bring peace to the dead and to restore happiness to the living.

MEMORY CHARM: This herb was among the first used to improve the conscious mind. Just smelling it before any mental endeavor is said to clear the mind and improve memory retention.

WOMAN'S RECLAIMING SPELL: Rosemary has always been considered a woman's herb that, when grown near the home, indicates a strong feminine presence within. So, if it's necessary to reclaim space from imposing guests or housemates, simply burn some rosemary while moving counterclockwise through the space saying, *"I reclaim this, my sacred space, here my magic shines, my energy saturates every space, to make this home truly mine."* Douse the incense and keep it somewhere safe in case you need to do spiritual housecleaning again.

SAFFRON

This herb is often considered a suitable offering to the gods because it is so rare. It takes over thirty thousand crocus flowers to make a mere ounce of saffron.

WIND CHARM: It is said that if you scatter saffron in the direction from which you wish a wind to come, the spirit of the spice will raise a gust and continue to blow until you bury some of the herb in the ground at the same spot.

APHRODISIAC OIL: The scent of saffron has long been trusted for helping inspire passion. For this, you can burn it as incense or add it to hot tea saying *"Ignite the fires within, as this spell begins. Like a flame to my heart, passion impart."*

SAGE

In Native American and many other indigenous traditions, sage is a favorite herb for clearing away negative vibrations.

INSECT REPELLANT CHARM: Sage effectively keeps away natural and spiritual pests in all shapes and sizes (including annoying people!). Wash your body in a tincture of sage water and keep a fresh or dried sprig with you.

Wisdom Spell: Take a handful of sage flowers and close your eyes. Focus on your desire to grow in wisdom saying *"Floral spirit by your name, my life will ne'er be the same. My will, my heart, pray now see, and bring back to me sagacity!"* Release all but a pinch of the herb to the Earth, and sprinkle the rest in your shoes so wisdom walks with you.

Tansy

The word *tansy* means "timeless," making this a lovely addition to the magical altar. Greek tradition says it was this herb that made Ganymede immortal.

Spirituality Charm: Early in Christian tradition a tansy cake represented the ceaseless nature of the human spirit. Carry a sprig of it dried in your pocket to keep you aware of your birthright as a citizen of all time.

Summerland Spell: It's not uncommon to see a sprig of tansy being used at Summerland Rituals to cleanse the circle. An incantation or invocation is usually added to this action. An example of an invocation is *"Round the circle, round and round. Today a spirit is homeward bound. From the Earth but momentarily torn, soon the spirit shall be reborn!"* Afterward, it is appropriate to leave the tansy sprig on the deceased's grave, or near their ashes.

Thyme

Persian cuisine incorporates thyme flowers in everything from soups to stuffings and vinegar. The Greeks used it as a favored herb to honor the gods.

Beauty Charm: According to ancient Roman custom, washing in thyme water will enhance your natural comeliness. To increase the effect, steep the herb in dew gathered on May Day morning.

Humor Spell: Since this herb is associated with the fairy folk, it has a whimsical nature. When you want to improve your sense of humor, steep some thyme in water and sprinkle it into your aura. Afterward, take a feather and move it clockwise throughout your aura to literally tickle yourself happy again.

Tulip

Tulips open at dawn and close by dusk, making them lovely solar emblems. These flowers are edible and make a fanciful cup for chicken or tuna salad.

Solar Charm: At dawn, gather a tulip that's just opening as you recite this incantation, *"At sunrise let my mind be keen, alert, and wise; at sunset, put the spell to rest."* Carry the flower with you until sunset, then bury the petals in the earth for a good night's sleep.

Prosperity Spell: Gather a handful of tulip seeds and scatter all but two to a Southerly wind saying *"Silver and gold, silver and gold, one to have and one to hold. To the winds fly, fall, and free, bring to me prosperity!"* Put the last two seeds in your wallet or purse to attract money.

Violet

In the Doctrine of Signatures, violets are known as "heart's ease" because of the heart-shaped leaf. In Christian lore, violets turned purple from drops of blood off the Cross.

Heartbreak Charm: To overcome sadness from unrequited love, carry a waxed or pressed violet close to your heart.

Peace Spell: Living violets are said to bring peace to both the living and the dead. Plant them wherever you want to be surrounded by tranquility saying *"Where these flowers are sown, bring peace. Where the blossoms abide, may calm never cease."*

There are so many other plants and flowers that a Green Witch could use in spells and charms that they could easily fill a book: oranges and olives, peas and pine, sandalwood and savory...While not all of these items exist in the Green Witch's garden or home, everything that nature gives us has potential for magic. It's just a matter of obtaining what we wish, then using it appropriately, adding personal vision and flair for more pleasing and powerful results.

So as you walk through supermarkets, spice shops, nature stores, or the forest, don't forget to see what wonders Gaia may have brought to those places. Store-bought or plucked fresh, Green Witches find magic in every bit of flora, and then happily weave that magic into their daily lives.

Fair Winds and Sweet Waters be yours...

Correspondence List

To provide a complete correspondence list for all the planet's magically-oriented flora would require a whole book. Many of the plants listed here have already been mentioned in the previous materials, but some have not. If what you're working with isn't listed here, I recommend any of the following titles to explore magical properties further: Paul Beyerl's *Herbal Magick*, Scott Cunningham's *Encyclopedia of Magical Herbs*, or my book, *The Herbal Arts*.

ALLSPICE

RULING PLANET: Mars
DEITIES: —
MAGICAL CORRESPONDENCE: Prosperity, Good Fortune
ELEMENT: Fire

ANISE

RULING PLANET: Jupiter, Moon
DEITIES: Hermes, Apollo
MAGICAL CORRESPONDENCE: Youth, Vitality, Sleep
ELEMENT: Air

APPLE

RULING PLANET: Venus, Jupiter
DEITIES: Aphrodite, Venus, Hera, Odin, Zeus
MAGICAL CORRESPONDENCE: Health, Relationships, Longevity, Fertility, Divination
ELEMENT: Water

BASIL

RULING PLANET: Mars
DEITIES: Vishnu, Krishna
MAGICAL CORRESPONDENCE: Loyalty, Adoration, Compassion, Prosperity
ELEMENT: Fire

BAY

RULING PLANET: Sun
DEITIES: Apollo, Ceres, Eros, Fides
MAGICAL CORRESPONDENCE: Success, Strength, Victory, Psychism
ELEMENT: Fire

BLACKBERRY

RULING PLANET: Venus
DEITIES: Brigit
MAGICAL CORRESPONDENCE: Protection, Health, Abundance
ELEMENT: Water

CATNIP

RULING PLANET: Venus
DEITIES: Bast
MAGICAL CORRESPONDENCE: Joy, Playfulness, Familiars (cats)
ELEMENT: Water

Celery

RULING PLANET: Mercury
DEITIES: —
MAGICAL CORRESPONDENCE: Awareness, Consciousness, Passion
ELEMENT: Fire

Chrysanthemum

RULING PLANET: Sun, Mercury
DEITIES: —
MAGICAL CORRESPONDENCE: Longevity, Protection
ELEMENT: Fire

Cinnamon

RULING PLANET: Sun
DEITIES: Venus
MAGICAL CORRESPONDENCE: Love, Purification, Vision
ELEMENT: Fire

Clove

RULING PLANET: Jupiter, Uranus
DEITIES: —
MAGICAL CORRESPONDENCE: Cleansing, Protection, Love, Abundance
ELEMENT: Fire

Corn

RULING PLANET: Moon
DEITIES: Corn Mother, Demeter, Mithra
MAGICAL CORRESPONDENCE: Safety, Providence, Fortune
ELEMENT: Earth

DAISY

RULING PLANET: Venus
DEITIES: Freya, Jupiter, Thor, Artemis
MAGICAL CORRESPONDENCE: Youth, Passion, Safety, Fairies
ELEMENT: Water

DANDELION

RULING PLANET: Jupiter
DEITIES: Hecate
MAGICAL CORRESPONDENCE: Psychism, Wind Magic, Wish
   Craft
ELEMENT: Air

DILL

RULING PLANET: Mercury
DEITIES: Horus
MAGICAL CORRESPONDENCE: Rest, Money, Passion
ELEMENT: Fire

FENNEL

RULING PLANET: Mercury
DEITIES: Adonis, Prometheus, Dionysus
MAGICAL CORRESPONDENCE: Alertness, Protection, Health
ELEMENT: Fire

GARDENIA

RULING PLANET: Moon
DEITIES: —
MAGICAL CORRESPONDENCE: Well-being, Peace, Spirituality
ELEMENT: Water

GARLIC

RULING PLANET: Mars
DEITIES: Hecate
MAGICAL CORRESPONDENCE: Protection, Healing, Banishing
ELEMENT: Fire

GERANIUM

RULING PLANET: Venus
DEITIES: —
MAGICAL CORRESPONDENCE: Safety, Strength, Hospitality
ELEMENT: Water

GINGER

RULING PLANET: Mars
DEITIES: —
MAGICAL CORRESPONDENCE: Energy, Victory, Prosperity
ELEMENT: Fire

HAWTHORN

RULING PLANET: Mars
DEITIES: Flora
MAGICAL CORRESPONDENCE: Love, Fertility
ELEMENT: Fire

HEATHER

RULING PLANET: Venus
DEITIES: Isis, Osiris
MAGICAL CORRESPONDENCE: Weather magic, Beauty, Fortune
ELEMENT: Water

HONEYSUCKLE

RULING PLANET: Jupiter
DEITIES: —
MAGICAL CORRESPONDENCE: Prosperity, Insight, Health
ELEMENT: Earth

HORSERADISH

RULING PLANET: Mars
DEITIES: —
MAGICAL CORRESPONDENCE: Purification, Protection
ELEMENT: Fire

IRIS

RULING PLANET: Venus
DEITIES: Iris, Hera, Juno
MAGICAL CORRESPONDENCE: Cleansing, Wisdom, Courage, Faith
ELEMENT: Water

LAVENDER

RULING PLANET: Mercury
DEITIES: Hecate, Saturn
MAGICAL CORRESPONDENCE: Peace, Safety, Cleansing, Fidelity
ELEMENT: Air

LEMON

RULING PLANET: Moon, Venus
DEITIES: —
MAGICAL CORRESPONDENCE: Cleansing, Love
ELEMENT: Water

LILY

RULING PLANET: Moon
DEITIES: Juno, Kwan Yin
MAGICAL CORRESPONDENCE: Goddess magic, Purity, Hex breaking
ELEMENT: Water

MARIGOLD

RULING PLANET: Sun
DEITIES: —
MAGICAL CORRESPONDENCE: Psychism, Legality, Consecration
ELEMENT: Fire

MARJORAM

RULING PLANET: Mercury
DEITIES: Aphrodite, Venus, Ilmarinen
MAGICAL CORRESPONDENCE: Love, Joy, Safety, Abundance
ELEMENT: Air

MINT

RULING PLANET: Venus
DEITIES: Pluto, Hecate
MAGICAL CORRESPONDENCE: Refreshment, Safe travel, Passion, Well-being
ELEMENT: Air

MUSTARD

RULING PLANET: Sun
DEITIES: Mars, Aesculapius
MAGICAL CORRESPONDENCE: Health, Conscious Mind, Fruitfulness
ELEMENT: Fire

MYRTLE

RULING PLANET: Venus
DEITIES: Aphrodite, Bon Dea, Hathor
MAGICAL CORRESPONDENCE: Abundance, Energy, Prosperity, Safety
ELEMENT: Water

NUTMEG

RULING PLANET: Jupiter
DEITIES: —
MAGICAL CORRESPONDENCE: Fortune, Prosperity, Devotion
ELEMENT: Fire

PARSLEY

RULING PLANET: Mercury
DEITIES: Persephone
MAGICAL CORRESPONDENCE: Security, Sensuality, Cleansing
ELEMENT: Air

PEAS

RULING PLANET: Venus, Jupiter
DEITIES: Nuba
MAGICAL CORRESPONDENCE: Wealth, Success, Love
ELEMENT: Earth

PERIWINKLE

RULING PLANET: Venus
DEITIES: —
MAGICAL CORRESPONDENCE: Passion, Abundance, Awareness, Protection
ELEMENT: Water

PINE

RULING PLANET: Mars
DEITIES: Pan, Sylvanus, Cybele, Poseidon
MAGICAL CORRESPONDENCE: Cleansing, Prosperity, Health,
Fertility
ELEMENT: Air

POTATO

RULING PLANET: Moon, Saturn
DEITIES: —
MAGICAL CORRESPONDENCE: Poppet magic, Healing
ELEMENT: Earth

PRIMROSE

RULING PLANET: Venus
DEITIES: Freya
MAGICAL CORRESPONDENCE: Safety, Fairies, Love
ELEMENT: Earth

ROSE

RULING PLANET: Venus
DEITIES: Aphrodite, Eros, Isis, Demeter, Bacchus
MAGICAL CORRESPONDENCE: Love, Magic, Psychism, Protec-
tion, Passion
ELEMENT: Water

ROSEMARY

RULING PLANET: Sun
DEITIES: —
MAGICAL CORRESPONDENCE: Remembrance, Love, Health,
Rest, and Energy
ELEMENT: Fire

Saffron

Ruling Planet: Sun
Deities: Eos, Amun Ra, Brahma
Magical Correspondence: Love, Prosperity, Strength, Mystical Insight
Element: Fire

Sage

Ruling Planet: Jupiter
Deities: Zeus
Magical Correspondence: Wisdom, Long life, Wishes
Element: Air

Sunflower

Ruling Planet: Sun
Deities: Apollo, Demeter
Magical Correspondence: Wish Craft, Fertility, Insight
Element: Fire

Tansy

Ruling Planet: Venus
Deities: —
Magical Correspondence: Well-being, Immortality
Element: Water

Tarragon

Ruling Planet: Mars
Deities: —
Magical Correspondence: Power, Zest
Element: Fire

Thyme

RULING PLANET: Venus
DEITIES: —
MAGICAL CORRESPONDENCE: Fairy sight, Sleep, Bravery, Health
ELEMENT: Water

Tulip

RULING PLANET: Venus
DEITIES: —
MAGICAL CORRESPONDENCE: Love, Safety, Abundance
ELEMENT: Earth

Vanilla

RULING PLANET: Venus
DEITIES: —
MAGICAL CORRESPONDENCE: Passion, Insight
ELEMENT: Water

Violet

RULING PLANET: Venus
DEITIES: Venus, Io, Zeus
MAGICAL CORRESPONDENCE: Good fortune, Tranquility, Unity, Healing, Wish Craft
ELEMENT: Water

Willow

RULING PLANET: Moon
DEITIES: Aino, Hera, Ceres, Hecate
MAGICAL CORRESPONDENCE: Magic, Flexibility
ELEMENT: Water

Abbreviated Bibliography

Beyerl, Paul. *Herbal Magick.* Phoenix Publishing, 1998.

Black, William George. *Folk Medicine.* Burt Franklin Co., 1883.

Bruce-Mitford, Miranda. *Illustrated Book of Signs and Symbols.* Dorling Kindersley Publishing, 1996.

Clarkson, Rosetta. *Golden Age of Herbs and Herbalists.* Dover Publishing, 1940.

Clarkson, Rosetta. *Herbs and Savory Seeds.* Dover Publishing, 1972.

Cunningham, Scott. *Cunningham's Encyclopedia of Magical Herbs.* Llewellyn Publications, 1985.

Fox, William. *Family Botanical Guide.* 18th ed., Sheffield, 1907.

Freethy, Ron. *Book of Plant Uses, Names and Folklores.* Tanager Books, 1985.

Gordon, Lesley. *Green Magic.* Viking Press, 1972.

Gordon, Stuart. *Encyclopedia of Myths and Legends.* Headline Book Publishing, 1993.

Griggs, Barbara. *History of Herbal Medicine.* Viking Press, 1981.

Hall, Manly P. *Secret Teachings of All Ages.* Philosophical Research, Society, 1977.

Hyton, W. H., editor. *Rodale's Illustrated Encyclopedia of Herbs.* Rodale Press, 1987.

Kieckhefer, Richard. *Magick in the Middle Ages.* Cambridge University Press, 1989.

Kraaz, Ingrid, and Wilfing Von Rohr. *The Healing Flower Color Card Set*. AGM Aktiengesellschaft Müller, 1990.

Leach, Maria, Jerome Fried, editors. *Standard Dictionary of Folklore, Mythology, and Legend*. Harper San Francisco, 1984.

LeStrange, Richard. *History of Herbal Plants*. Arco Publishing, 1977.

Lurker, Manfred. *Dictionary of Gods and Goddesses, Devils and Demons*. Routledge & Kegan Paul Ltd., 1987.

MacNicol, Mary. *Flower Cookery*. Fleet Press Corporation, 1967.

Matthews, John, editor. *World Atlas of Divination*. Bulfinch Press, 1992.

McLean, Teresa. *Medieval English Gardens*. Viking Press, 1980.

Murray, Colin, and Liz Murray. *The Celtic Tree Oracle: A System of Divination*. Macmillan, 1988.

Northcote, Rosalind. *Book of Herb Lore*. Dover Publishing, 1912.

Potterton, David, editor. *Culpeper's Herbal*. Sterling Publishing, 1983.

Quinly, *Cariel. Crop Circle Cards, The Living Oracle*. Sacred Mas Productions, 1998.

Rhode, Eleanor Sinclair. *Olde English Herbals*. Dover Publishing, 1922.

Roberts, Annie Lise. *Cornucopia*. Knickerbocker Press, 1998.

Ryan, Mark, and Chesca Potter. *The Greenwood Tarot: Pre-Celtic Shamanism of the Mythic Forest*. Thorsons Pub., 1996.

Schapira, David, et al. *Book of Coffee and Tea*. St. Martin's Press, 1906.

Singer, Charles. *From Magick to Science*. Dover Publishing, 1928.

Telesco, Patricia. *A Kitchen Witch's Cookbook*. Llewellyn Publications, 1994.

——. *Herbal Arts*. Citadel Press, 1998.

——. *Labyrinth Walking*. Citadel Press, 2001.

——. *Victorian Flower Oracle*. Llewellyn Publications, 1994.

Thistleton-Dyer, T. F. *The Folk-Lore of Plants*. D. Appleton & Co., 1889.

Tierra, Michael and V.D. Zlomanov. *The Herbal Tarot*. U.S. Games Systems, Inc., 2002.

Index

G

More From Crossed Crow Books

A Victorian Grimoire by Patricia Telesco
The Way of Four by Deborah Lipp
Magic of the Elements by Deborah Lipp
Witchcraft on a Shoestring by Deborah Blake
Circle, Coven, & Grove by Deborah Blake
Merlin: Master of Magick by Gordon Strong
The Bones Fall in a Spiral by Mortellus
Your Star Sign by Per Henrik Gullfoss
The Complete Book of Spiritual Astrology by Per Henrik Gullfoss
Icelandic Plant Magic by Albert Bjorn
The Black Book of Johnathan Knotbristle by Chris Allaun
A Witch's Book of Terribles by Wycke Malliway
In the Shadow of Thirteen Moons by Kimberly Sherman-Cook
Witchcraft Unchained by Craig Spencer
Wiccan Mysteries by Raven Grimassi
Wiccan Magick by Raven Grimassi
Celtic Tree Mysteries by Steve Blamires
Star Magic by Sandra Kynes
Witches' Sabbats and Esbats by Sandra Kynes
A Spirit Work Primer by Naag Loki Shivanaath
A Witch's Shadow Magick Compendium by Raven Digitalis
Flight of the Firebird by Kenneth Johnson
Witchcraft and the Shamanic Journey by Kenneth Johnson
Travels Through Middle Earth by Alaric Albertsson
Be Careful What You Wish For by Laetitia Latham-Jones
Death's Head by Blake Malliway
The Wildwood Way by Cliff Seruntine

Learn more at
www.CrossedCrowBooks.com